Also by David Bach
available from
Random House Large Print

Start Late, Finish Rich

THE
AUTOMATIC
MILLIONAIRE
HOMEOWNER™

A Powerful Plan to
Finish Rich in Real Estate

DAVID BACH

RANDOM HOUSE
LARGE PRINT

personal finances and specific to the individual should be addressed to an appropriate professional to ensure that the situation has been evaluated carefully and appropriately. The Author and Publisher specifically disclaim any liability, loss, or risk that is incurred as a consequence, directly or indirectly, of the use and application of any of the contents of this work.

The Library of Congress has established a Cataloging-in-Publication record for this title.

ISBN-13: 978-0-7393-2579-7
ISBN-10: 0-7393-2579-5

www.randomlargeprint.com

FIRST LARGE PRINT EDITION

10 9 8 7 6 5 4 3 2 1

This Large Print edition published in accord with the standards of the N.A.V.H.

To the millions of readers of the
FinishRich books and
The Automatic Millionaire:
Thank you for your feedback,
your encouragement, your letters and
e-mails, and your success stories.
You inspire me and our team at
FinishRich Media to do what we do.

CONTENTS

THE AUTOMATIC MILLIONAIRE HOMEOWNER™

INTRODUCTION

What if I told you the smartest investment you would ever make during your lifetime would be a home?

What if I told you that the way in which you buy your homes over the course of your lifetime would determine whether you ever become rich?

What if I told you that in just an hour or two I could share with you a simple system that would help you become rich through homeownership?

What if I told you that this system was called the Automatic Millionaire Homeowner—and that if you spent an hour or two with me, you could learn how to become one?

Would you be interested? Would you be willing to spend a few hours with me? Would you like to become an Automatic Millionaire Homeowner?

—DAVID BACH

If the lines above got your attention, then please keep reading. Stay where you are for a few minutes and read just a few more pages. Whether you rent or own, this book can transform your life. It's a powerfully simple plan—a lifelong strategy for wealth-building that works in any market because it's based on time-tested wisdom that is tried and true.

THE AMERICAN DREAM
IS BACK!

Over the last few years, something radical happened to the way Americans think about money and investing—something so radical that it may have forever changed the way we live our lives and plan for our futures. What happened is that a lot of people got fed up with the stock market.

The reason for this change of heart was simple. Between March 2000 and the summer of 2002, the U.S. stock market imploded, with losses totaling a whopping $6.9 trillion. To say the least, it was one brutal meltdown. And its effects lingered for years. By the middle of 2005, the NASDAQ Composite Index, which tracks mainly high-tech stocks, was still more than 40 percent below where it had been in 2000, while the blue-chip Dow Jones Industrial Average remained down more than 10 percent.

For many families—maybe yours was one of them—this market "correction" (which is what the experts called it) was the proverbial straw that broke the camel's back. Americans simply decided that enough was enough. They were taking their stock market "chips" and going home—literally and figuratively.

Instead of keeping their money in stocks, many Americans started investing in real estate—mainly in homes, home improvements, and second homes. This simple change has led to a boom in real estate and homeownership the likes of which we've never seen before. It's an exciting time to be building wealth in America, but it's also a frightening time because Americans now have so much of their wealth tied up in their homes—about $10 trillion in equity, the Federal Reserve reported in 2005, or about the same amount as there is in stocks. And many people are wondering—maybe you're one of them—whether this is a safe place to be.

SMART HOMEOWNERS ARE FINISHING RICH—HOW ABOUT YOU?

Between 2001 and 2005, the average homeowner saw the value of his house jump by more than 50 percent. Many homeowners doubled, tripled, and in some cases even quadrupled their wealth in just five years because of exploding real estate values. As prices soared, experts began warning that the real estate market was starting to look like the overheated technology market of the late 1990s. Nonetheless, as I write, the gold rush to real estate continues.

According to the National Association of Realtors, the median home price in America hit $220,000 in August 2005—a more than

55 percent increase in less than five years. And that was just the median. In many markets, including San Francisco, Las Vegas, Miami, San Diego, and New York, home prices shot up more than 100 percent in the same period. Some people were literally able to buy a home, live in it for five years, then sell it and retire. Done. Game over.

Imagine that. Buy a home, live in it, build your wealth, get great tax deductions—and then retire rich. It may sound too good to be true. But it's not. It has happened—and it will continue to happen for millions of people over the next few decades. The question is, will it happen for you? Will you catch this wave, miss it—or will it crash on you?

BOOM OR BUST—YOU CAN STILL MAKE MONEY IN REAL ESTATE

As I sit here in August 2005, I have no idea when you will be reading what I'm writing. Maybe it's March 2006 (when this book is scheduled to be published)—by which time the real estate market could be slowing or cooling down to modest single-digit annual gains (or not). Perhaps this book was bought by a friend of yours who passed it along to you—and it's now 2007 and those once "certain" boom markets are going bust due to speculation. Or maybe the opposite has happened—interest rates have remained at historic lows, and home prices have continued their march upward.

In fact, it doesn't really matter when you happen to be reading this or what's going on right now in the markets. This book is not about the boom . . . or the busts. It's not about timing the real estate market. It's not about the fantasy of "getting rich overnight" in real estate.

What this book is about is the truth. And the truth is this:

Nothing you will ever do in your lifetime is likely to make you as much money as buying a home and living in it.

Realistically, the best investment you will ever make will be your home.

Don't worry about timing the market in real estate. It's time **in** the market that will matter for you.

HOMEOWNERS GET RICH AND RENTERS STAY POOR

The bottom line is this: The American Dream of building a nest egg by owning a home is no fantasy. Homeowners have been getting rich off their real estate for years, and they will continue to do so in the future. There are also more of them than ever before. In fact, as I write this, there are a record 73.4 million homeowners in the United States—more than 69 percent of American families, according to government statistics. And it's not just wealthy people who are buying homes. More people under the age of 25 are buying homes than ever before, and for the first time ever a majority of minority Americans are homeowners.

The same thing is happening all over the

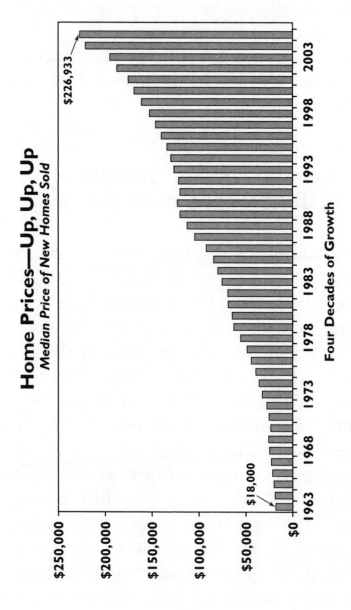

Home Prices—Up, Up, Up
Median Price of New Homes Sold

$226,933

$18,000

Four Decades of Growth

Data for 2005 is through September and is preliminary.
Source: U.S. Census Bureau (October 27, 2005)

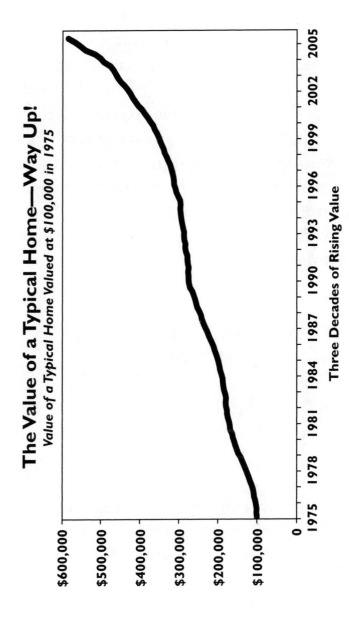

The Value of a Typical Home—Way Up!
Value of a Typical Home Valued at $100,000 in 1975

Three Decades of Rising Value

Data for 2005 is through the second quarter.
Source: Office of Federal Housing Enterprise Oversight (September 1, 2005)

world. According to a report in **The Economist** magazine, the total value of residential property in developed countries has soared in recent years, rising from $40 trillion to $70 trillion. The fact is, never before have so many people in so many countries seen housing prices rise so much for so long.

If owning a home is working so well, what's not working? The first answer is renting. For renters, the facts are frankly a little depressing.

IF YOU WANT TO BE RICH, DON'T RENT

I apologize up front if you're a renter, because I know this may be brutal to hear, but you have to hear it if you're going to change. So here goes.

You simply can't get rich renting. We know this. It's a timeless truth. According to a recent report by the Federal Reserve, the average renter in America is basically broke. **Try this on for size:**

- In 2003 (the most recent year for which this kind of data is available), the average renter in America was worth less than $5,000.
- The average homeowner was worth nearly $172,000.

The comparison is pretty stunning. **The average homeowner is more than 34 TIMES RICHER than the average renter.**
Could it be any clearer?

The point is that if you're renting, it's time to stop. Not that there's anything wrong with people who rent. Renters aren't bad people. In fact, my goal for you is to someday own some homes or condos that you can rent to other people. It's just that if you are a renter yourself, I don't want you to continue being one much longer.

LET'S TAKE A JOURNEY TOGETHER—AND SEE HOW EASY THIS CAN BE

This book is the eighth one I've written in the FinishRich Series; as of this writing, there are more than 4 million copies of these books in print, translated into 15 languages. If this is the first FinishRich book you've gotten, let me start by saying "thank you" for the opportunity to be your money guide and coach. If you are a returning reader, let me also say a sincere "thank you" for your trust in me.

Writing these books has been an amazing journey for me. Each and every day, my team and I at FinishRich Media receive letters and e-mails from readers sharing with us how they've taken to heart the messages and lessons they've read in my books and used them to change their lives for the better.

WHY THIS BOOK NOW?

Back in January 2004, I published a little book called **The Automatic Millionaire**, which immediately became a #1 **New York Times** and international bestseller. That month, I also had the incredible opportunity to share my book's simple message on **The Oprah Winfrey Show.** Our goal on **Oprah** was to teach millions of viewers how easy it could be to become an Automatic Millionaire by "paying yourself first" and making all your savings automatic. No budget was needed, no discipline was required. All it would take to achieve real wealth over your lifetime was a simple program that anyone could set up in an hour.

One section of **The Automatic Millionaire**—and also one of my appearances on **Oprah**—focused on real estate, making the point that after "paying yourself first," the most important thing you could do to achieve wealth was to buy a home. This prompted literally tens of thousands of readers to ask me the same question: "But how do I buy a home?" Others wrote, "I own a home but I don't feel rich. How do I use my home to become a millionaire?"

That's why I wrote this book.

MY MISSION WITH THIS BOOK IS TO HELP YOU USE HOMEOWNERSHIP TO BUILD REAL WEALTH FOR LIFE— AUTOMATICALLY!

For many of our parents and grandparents, real estate is a safety net. The equity in their houses is the cushion that supports them financially during retirement.

But I have a different—and better—plan for you. **Automatic Millionaire Homeowners are proactive.** They look at their homes not just as potential safety nets but as the means to live and get rich. That's my goal for you.

My mission with this book is to show you how homeownership can be the centerpiece of your wealth-building strategy,

the key to achieving financial independence. Like **The Automatic Millionaire,** this book is designed to be read in just a few hours. In the process, you will learn everything you need to know, quickly and simply, to become an Automatic Millionaire Homeowner.

If you don't already own a home, I will take you by the hand and lead you step-by-step through the process of going from renting to homeownership. And once you become a homeowner—or if you already are one—I'll show you how to use your property to build wealth. Remember, when you purchase a home you're doing more than just buying a place to live in. You're creating an opportunity for true financial independence. If done properly, homeownership can be a foundation on which you can build real wealth—even if you never earn more than an ordinary income. Real estate has always been the leading tool people have used to build wealth in America—and it is not too late for it to work for you.

Most important, I'm going to share with

you how to make your homebuying experience as "automatic" as possible. In particular, I'll show you how to automate your mortgage payments so you can build equity in your home faster—increasing your net worth and opening a whole new world of possibilities for you. Ultimately, this little trick will enable you to become debt-free years ahead of schedule—which could save you more than $100,000 in mortgage interest and possibly even help you retire five to ten years early.

IT'S NEVER TOO LATE TO CATCH THE REAL ESTATE WAVE

"But, David, are you sure it's not too late?"

As I've traveled around the world in recent years doing television and radio shows, seminars, readings, and book signings, I've had the honor of meeting tens of thousands of readers. And at every event, speech, and airport encounter, I get asked the same questions. "David, what about real estate?" "Is it too late for me?" "Can I still buy a home?" "What type of mortgage should I use?" "What about buying a second home?" "My friend is investing in condos in Florida and flipping them. What do you think about that?" "My home has doubled in value in the last five years. Should I sell it and cash out?"

In fact, well over half the questions I get these days are about real estate. Given the spectacular performance of the real estate market over the last few years, this really isn't very surprising. Nonetheless, the questions remain.

Is it too late for you to catch this real estate wave? Or, as was the case with the stock market in the late 1990s, are we experiencing a bubble that's about to pop?

The answers to these questions will be found in this book. But I can tell you one thing right now: There's no reason to worry that homeownership will turn out to have been nothing more than a passing fad. And here's why:

AS LONG AS YOU'RE ALIVE, YOU HAVE TO LIVE SOMEWHERE

Read that again. **"As long as you're alive, you have to live somewhere."**

This is one of those facts of life that's so obvious we don't even think about it. Everybody has to live somewhere, and someone owns every place where someone lives. It may be your parents, or a landlord, or the government—but someone has owned every place where you and every one of your neighbors have lived.

Why shouldn't that someone be you?

HOW THIS BOOK WORKS

Every time the real estate markets take off, publishers pump out what seems like thousands of books and tapes on "how to get rich in real estate." Chances are, you've bought some of these books or tapes yourself. I know I have. Some of them are truly inspiring, but few of them give you a real plan.

They say you should own real estate if you want to be rich—but they don't tell you how. And many of them advocate unrealistic schemes that take so much work you'd practically have to quit your day job to put them into practice.

If you've read any of my other books in the FinishRich Series™, you know I don't do that. I want to inspire you to act, but I also want you to know and understand **exactly** what you need to do. And I make it simple—simple enough for you to be able to act quickly.

My books are about taking action— because it's action that ultimately will change your life.

So let's get started on our journey.

First, you're going to meet the "original" Automatic Millionaire Homeowner. In my years of being a financial advisor, author, and speaker, I've actually met thousands of Automatic Millionaire Homeowners. In fact, I've met more people who have become rich through real estate and homeownership than through any other means.

Lately, of course, it's become hard to

avoid people who like to brag about the money they've made in real estate. In fact, it's often the main topic of conversation at cocktail parties, and to me that's worrisome. The people you hear bragging about buying and "flipping" properties are just like the folks who bragged about their "dot-com" stocks in the late 1990s. Many of them are probably over-leveraged and are bound to get hurt financially. Some will lose their homes to foreclosure and, worse, may even end up bankrupt.

This book is not about how to be like those people. In fact, it's the opposite. It's about how to keep from getting sucked into the "buzz of a boom" and making foolish decisions—in short, how to become an Automatic Millionaire Homeowner who builds real wealth through a lifetime of homeownership.

These "average" homeowner millionaires are all around you, and there is no reason why you can't become one yourself. John and Lucy Martin, whom you're going to meet in the first chapter, are just such a success story. I met them about ten years ago and through their example realized how simple homeownership can make anyone rich—if you have a plan to make it happen.

The Martins' story did more than educate me. It inspired me to take action, to try to do what they had done. As a result, in just ten years I've increased my net worth by more than $1 million simply through homebuying.

Not bad considering I've only bought three homes so far in my life. So read their story and let it sink in. It's designed to open up your thinking—and inspire you to become an Automatic Millionaire Homeowner yourself. In the ten chapters that follow the Martins' story, I'll give you step-by-step instructions on exactly how to put yourself on the path to riches they took, teaching you how to transform yourself from a renter to a homeowner—and from a homeowner to an **Automatic Millionaire Homeowner.**

YOU DON'T HAVE TO DO THIS YOURSELF

From the outside, the real estate game can seem complicated and competitive, filled with lots of players, all of whom are striving to win. Because of this, many people simply give up on being a homeowner. Or if they become a homeowner, they never take the next step and buy a second home or a rental property.

My goal with this book is to show you how easy it can be to find your way through this seemingly complicated world. I'll explain what all these players really do and teach you how to pick good ones who can help you on your journey to becoming an Automatic Millionaire Homeowner. I'll translate the jargon real estate professionals use. Once you speak their language—and know what questions to ask—none of it will seem so intimidating.

ALMOST ANYONE CAN
BUY A HOME TODAY

You may think that if you've got a bad credit record, a lot of credit card debt, or not enough cash for a down payment, there's no way you could buy a home. If so, you'd be wrong. In fact, you wouldn't believe how easy it is for almost anyone to buy a home today, especially first-time homebuyers. There are programs set up specifically to help people who have no money for a down payment. There are national banks that will loan you more than 100 percent of the cost of a home. And there are institutions that will structure loans so that your monthly mortgage payment will be the same as the rent you may be paying right now.

If any of this seems confusing—or too good to be true—**don't worry**.

The fact is that homebuying is both easier and more straightforward than most people realize. Not only do both the government and the banks want you to become a homeowner, but thanks to the Internet you can shop for a loan, find a real estate agent, and search for available properties without ever leaving your couch. And in this book, I'll show you how to do it all.

THE PHILOSOPHY BEHIND THE AUTOMATIC MILLIONAIRE HOMEOWNER

- You can't get rich renting.
- You don't need a lot of money for a down payment on a home.
- You don't need good credit to buy a home.
- You should buy a home even if you have credit card debt.
- By adopting what I call the "Automatic Millionaire Mindset," you can build a fortune by buying just a few homes over the course of a lifetime.
- Homeowners get rich; landlords get **really** rich.
- **Above all, you need an "automatic system" to keep your real estate plan on track and guarantee that you won't fail.**

To make things even easier, this book is more interactive than any I've ever written. Each chapter ends with a short summary outline I call the Automatic Millionaire Homeowner Action Steps. These steps are your "ready, set, go" exercises—point-by-point instructions that you can use to make progress quickly toward your dream of homeownership and becoming an Automatic Millionaire Homeowner.

In addition, each chapter offers you a link to our web site at **www.finishrich.com**, where you can download—for free—a series of special audio programs that contain even more information to help you become an Automatic Millionaire Homeowner.

So let's get started. Let's take a look at how John and Lucy Martin became Automatic Millionaire Homeowners, and then let's go look at how you can do the same.

In just a few hours, I believe you'll be surprised by how much your thinking can change. And as your thinking changes, you'll begin to see—as thousands of people already have—that you can do it, too.

FREE! AUTOMATIC MILLIONAIRE HOMEOWNER PROGRAM

Each book I write contains a gift. It's my way of saying "thank you" for allowing me to become your money coach. This book offers more than one gift—it comes with a complete audio program designed to follow the book interactively. It's called THE AUTOMATIC MILLIONAIRE HOMEOWNER PROGRAM, and you'll find the entire program at **www.finishrich.com/ homeowner**.

The web address leads to a podcast that you can listen to in conjunction with the chapter or at some later time that's more convenient. Also at this area of the web site, you'll find special tools designed to help you achieve your dream of becoming an Automatic Millionaire Homeowner. And you'll be able to read real-life success stories of people like you who are implementing the Automatic Millionaire philosophies into their daily lives.

In all, this program has a value of more than $295. But it's free, as my gift to you—so take advantage of it and enjoy!

CHAPTER ONE

MEETING THE AUTOMATIC MILLIONAIRE HOMEOWNER

I'll never forget when I met my first Automatic Millionaire Homeowner. I was in my late twenties and was on one of my first book tours, giving a talk at a bookstore in San Jose, California.

After a long down period, the real estate market in California was starting to take off, and many of the people who had come to see me had questions about whether now was a good time to buy property. In the middle of discussing the benefits of home-ownership, I called on a young woman named Karen, who seemed particularly excited. "David," she asked, "what do you think about the idea of setting up an LLC for real estate? I'm trying to decide if I should put my property investments into an LLC or a Nevada corporation."

An LLC, by the way, is a Limited Liability Corporation. Don't worry if you don't know what this is. Neither did Karen when she asked the question.

I told Karen there was no simple answer to her question. "It depends," I said. "What type of real estate do you own?"

Karen blushed a little, then said, "Actually, I don't own any yet, but I just read a book on real estate that said I should put my real estate in an LLC or Nevada corporation, because then my assets would be protected against frivolous lawsuits." She shrugged helplessly. "It all sounded so complicated. I'm not sure where to start."

"Well, let me ask you something else," I replied. "Do you have a lot of assets right now?"

Karen shook her head. "Not really."

I smiled at her. "You just read a book on real estate," I said. "Why? Is it owning real estate that matters to you or the financial freedom you're hoping to get from it?"

"The financial freedom," Karen said firmly. "I want to get out of debt, stop renting, and finally get ahead. I'm tired of living paycheck to paycheck."

"That's great. Congratulations on knowing what you want and making a decision to get there. You've already done the hard part—something that most people never do. Now, how about we focus on it one step at a time? Instead of worrying about whether or not you need a complicated LLC structure for your assets, let's look at how you would go from renting to homeownership. That's really your first step in building assets."

Karen nodded enthusiastically. "I know," she said. "My parents told me that I should focus on buying a home. The book I read said I should look at foreclosures and buy real estate with no money down. But the book didn't really explain how to do it. It just said rich people do this all the time."

LEARNING FROM THE REAL WORLD OF REAL PEOPLE

I knew the book Karen was talking about. At the time, it was very popular and I had read it myself. It contained some valuable ideas and information, so I didn't want to single it out. Instead, I looked around at the audience and asked, "How many of you have seen one of those 'No Money Down' real estate infomercials?"

There were more than 100 people in the room and pretty much all of them raised their hands.

"Great," I said. "Now, how many of you have actually bought a property with no money down?"

Out of the 100 people there, two raised their hands.

"OK, so we know it's not impossible to buy real estate with no money down. But we also know it's not very common, nor is it necessarily easy. Now, how many of you own property and have it in an LLC or Nevada corporation?"

Not one hand went up.

"Interesting," I said. "Here's another question for you. How many of you own your own homes or condos?"

About half the audience raised their hands.

"For those of you who own a home or condo, keep your hand up if it's the best investment you ever made."

Nearly every hand that was already up stayed up.

"OK, keep your hands up and let me put a question to the rest of you who don't own your own homes. How many of you have had your parents or grandparents tell you that their home was their best investment they ever made?"

Now, nearly EVERY single hand in the room was raised.

"Isn't that interesting?" I said. "What we just did was conduct a real-life test on real people about what seems to work in the real world. And you know what we've learned? We've learned that there's a lot of 'razzle-dazzle' out there in real estate. 'Buy real estate with no money down.' 'Protect your assets with an LLC.' It's not that you can't do these things. It's that they're not what you should be focusing on.

"What we've just seen is that there is one thing that is being done over and over again that works like a charm consistently—and that is buying a home and owning it for a while."

I turned back to Karen, who smiled and laughed. "Okay, I get it," she said. "Stop renting and buy a home! That seems to make a lot of sense. Now if you could just help me with the down payment, I'd be all set."

The audience laughed.

"I've got a better idea," I said, laughing along with them. "How about I teach you how to save up the money you'll need for a down payment and how to get the financing you'll need from the bank. The truth is that there are many special loan programs for first-time homebuyers that can help you buy a place faster than you'd think."

Karen's smile widened. "Sounds good to me!" she said.

THE MOST IMPORTANT INVESTMENT YOU WILL EVER MAKE IS YOUR HOME

As Karen sat down, I caught sight of an older couple I had spotted earlier in the back of the room. They were sitting there with their arms crossed. When you're speaking to an audience, crossed arms are usually a bad sign, but these two folks were both nodding and smiling.

After the question-and-answer session ended, I spent twenty minutes or so signing copies of my book. To my surprise, I noticed the older couple patiently waiting for me to finish. When I finally did, they came up to me. "David," said the man, "do you have a few minutes for us to share a story with you?"

"Absolutely," I replied. "All my books are based on the stories of real people. I love to listen—and learn."

"WE'RE MILLIONAIRES BECAUSE OF THE HOMES WE BOUGHT"

Their names were John and Lucy Martin. They looked to be in their early sixties, but young for their ages—fit and athletic—and excited about life.

"I hope you won't take this wrong," John began, "but we didn't actually come to the bookstore to hear you speak. We were just browsing when we heard the commotion in the back and thought we'd check it out. You were really engaging, so we decided to stay and listen."

"You were right with the advice you gave that young woman Karen," Lucy piped in. "A house **is** the best investment you'll ever make."

"And renting never makes sense if you can avoid it," John added.

John and Lucy looked at each other and smiled. "We know from personal experience," said John. "In fact, we're millionaires today because of the homes we bought over the years."

"Really?" I said.

"Now don't misunderstand," John continued. "I don't mean to boast. It's just that I think it's really frightening how many of these young kids seem to be making so much money in the stock market so quickly. They don't realize that all those dot-com profits are just on paper—and that until they sell their stock and invest in something like a home, it's nothing but pure speculation." This was the 1990s, and John was wise to be skeptical.

"WHAT MADE US RICH WAS HOMEOWNERSHIP"

Lucy nodded vigorously. "We've invested in the stock market ourselves over the years, but we've always been well-diversified and in it for the long haul," she said.

I nodded in agreement.

"But here's the thing," Lucy went on, "what made us rich was being homeowners. When we were young, we never thought we'd be able to even buy a home. But it turned out to be so much easier than we imagined—and ultimately it helped us build real financial security."

John beamed proudly. "I still find it hard to believe, but we own more than $3 million worth of real estate. And we've done it simply by buying a handful of homes, living in them, and being smart about which ones we kept as rentals and which ones we sold for a tax-free profit. To tell the truth, it's been fun."

"And so much easier than we imagined," added Lucy. "Can we tell you how we did it? We'll take you out for a latte!"

We all laughed. In the presentation the Martins had just sat through, I'd been talking about what I call The Latte Factor®, a concept of mine that explains how the small things we spend money on (like lattes) can end up costing us a fortune—or make you rich if you learn to cut them out and pay yourself first.

So we headed off to a coffee shop—and a lesson about how to get rich through home-ownership.

GETTING ON THE HOMEBUYING TRACK

John did most of the talking, but the story he told was definitely a joint effort. If anything, Lucy seemed to be the one who had originally gotten them on the homebuying track.

"We actually didn't buy our first home until we were in our late twenties," John started off. "And truth be told, we didn't really give much thought to money. I was in the military at the time and wasn't making much. But we weren't spending a lot either, because we lived on a base in Oakland and a lot of our living costs were covered. One thing that definitely helped was that the military had a bill-paying system where you could elect to have money taken out of your paycheck automatically. Basically, we saved money **automatically,** just the way you preached in your talk. We had a car we were paying for, so I had them take out the money for that. Then one day it was paid off, and we started discussing what to do with the extra cash that had been going to our car payments.

"It was Lucy's idea that we start saving for a house. My response was, 'Why should we save for a house when we can live on the base for practically nothing?' But Lucy insisted. She said that owning our own house would give us options. Renting would keep us trapped.

"Thank goodness I listened to her. Within two years, we had saved enough for a down payment."

"Don't make it sound so simple," Lucy interrupted with a smile. "Even then you weren't sure, were you, honey?"

John grinned back. "No, I wasn't," he admitted. "Our car was getting old, and I was in the mood for a new one. But Lucy put her foot down. She said, 'No way. We're not wasting this money on a new car. We're going to go look for a house.'"

"That's right," Lucy agreed. "We were starting a family, and I told him we needed to move off the base and find us a nice neighborhood with a good school system."

THE NEIGHBORHOOD WASN'T IDEAL, BUT THE HOUSE WAS AFFORDABLE

John resumed the story. "At first, it seemed pretty impossible. As we began looking, we quickly realized that we couldn't afford very much. It was hard because we'd both grown up in nice homes. Our parents certainly weren't rich, but things were cheaper in their day. The homes we were being shown were insanely expensive.

"To make matters worse, our friends were giving us a hard time for wanting to leave the base, telling us we were wasting our time. But Lucy was relentless. Every Sunday, we pored through the paper to see what was out there. We went to open houses on weekends and drove around neighborhoods we liked looking for 'For Sale' signs. But the more we looked, the more depressed we became. It seemed like nothing was in our price range in the places where we wanted to live.

"We were about to give up when we saw

an article in the paper about this area called Walnut Creek. Back then, Walnut Creek was in the middle of nowhere, in the absolute boondocks. But the houses were affordable, and the schools were good, and more and more young couples were moving out there.

"We called a real estate agent in the area and went out looking with her. In two days, we found a home for $30,000. Now, Walnut Creek really wasn't where we wanted to live. It was about twenty minutes farther out than we wanted to be. And the house wasn't perfect. It was small and it needed a lot of sweat equity, as they say. But it had three bedrooms and two baths, and we felt we could afford it. We had enough saved for a down payment, and we felt that with a lot of belt-tightening we could make the mortgage payments. Still, back then, $30,000 seemed like a fortune to us."

"YOU START SMALL AND YOU WORK YOUR WAY UP"

"While we were looking at the house, Lucy noticed I wasn't too excited about it. I think I even said to her, 'You know, this isn't exactly the dream house we've always talked about.' And she said, 'John, dreams start small.' And then our real estate agent said something I've never forgotten. She said, **'You don't buy your dream house with your first purchase, but it will be your first house that someday helps you get your dream house.'**

"We realized she was right, and then and there Lucy and I made the decision to go for it. We made an offer and it got accepted."

A $30,000 INVESTMENT EVENTUALLY TURNS INTO $1 MILLION

John leaned back in his chair, a faraway look in his eye as he recalled that fateful day. "That was nearly 35 years ago," he said. "Today, that little house is worth nearly a million dollars. I know because we still own it."

"We paid off the mortgage years ago," Lucy chimed in, "and we rent it now to a nice young couple with kids. They pay us nearly $3,000 a month. Hard to believe we bought it for less than it now brings us in rent in a single year."

"Our second house was a lot more expensive," John said, resuming the story. "It cost us a little over $100,000. Of course, it was bigger and it was in a new development—with a pool!"

"We needed both the space and the pool," Lucy laughed. "By then, we had three kids."

"And even though I was out of the service by then and making a little more money, we once again had to stretch to make the purchase," John continued. "But—and this is really important—we didn't stretch too much to buy it. In fact, we actually stretched a little **less** than we could afford because we had decided not to sell our first house but, instead, to keep it and rent it out.

So instead of selling, we refinanced just enough to pull out a down payment on our new place."

SAVING A TON OF MONEY BY PAYING OFF THE MORTGAGE EARLY

"By the time our kids went off to college, our $100,000 house was worth more than $500,000. We truly couldn't believe it."

"And best of all," Lucy added, "it was nearly paid off because we had used a program our bank offered called a 'biweekly mortgage payment plan.' It sounds complicated but it's not. What it does is help you pay off your mortgage extra fast, which saves you tons of money in interest."

"You know the saying, 'Time is money'?" John interjected. "Well, with mortgages, that's really true."

"Which is why in addition to using the biweekly mortgage payment plan, we also added a little extra to our mortgage payment at the end of the year when John got his bonus," said Lucy.

John nodded and gestured to Lucy. "Why don't you tell the rest of the story, hon?"

Lucy plunged ahead. "With our kids out of college, we really didn't need to worry about school systems anymore. John wanted to live on a golf course, and so we started looking around at golf communities."

"WE DID SOMETHING CRAZY—WE BOUGHT OUR DREAM HOUSE!"

"Long story short, we sold our second home for $650,000. And then we did something crazy with the money—we used it to buy our dream house! It was 4,000 square feet, with a pool. The price was $750,000, so once again we had to stretch a bit. But interest rates had come down a lot and we felt we could make the payments.

"We couldn't believe it. Little us, now living in a huge house, almost a mansion. It was nearly five times the size of our first house and three times the size of the houses we grew up in. Our kids thought we were crazy. But we were ready for some fun."

"Still are!" exclaimed John, and we all laughed.

"Well, that was ten years ago," Lucy went on. "We recently sold that house for more than $2 million. We spent part of the money on a new house on a golf course in Arizona, which is where we live now, and the rest to buy a small apartment building. The building has four units and makes us about $50,000 a year in rent after expenses. Between our first house, which we rent out, and this four-plex, we earn $90,000 a year. Not bad for a retired couple."

LIVING IT UP WITH NO FINANCIAL WORRIES

"And you know the most amazing thing about it all?" John asked. "We really didn't do anything all that special. But here we are 35 years later living it up, retired with no financial worries and a wonderful home on a golf course."

"Oh, come on," I said, "you're selling yourselves short. What you did really **was** special."

John shook his head. "Not at all. We always took care not to overextend ourselves. If we did anything at all special it was not to sell our first home. Renting out that house helped us build equity at someone else's expense. And ultimately, the rent from that house helped us pay down the mortgage on the house we were living in much faster. Because of that, when we were ready to buy our third home, we were able to afford a really big one."

"And when the tax laws changed," Lucy jumped in, "we really made out." She was referring to the changes Congress enacted in 1997. Before then, the government let homeowners sell a house once in their lifetimes without having to pay any taxes on the profits. But in 1997, Congress changed the rules. Now, every time you sell your house, the first $250,000 in profits are tax-free—the first $500,000, if you're a married couple.

"So when we sold our $750,000 California home for $2 million, $500,000 of the profit we made was tax-free," John explained. "We plan to do even better with our home in Arizona. We're going to sell it as soon as its value increases by $500,000 and lock in the tax-free gains again."

"EVEN IF OUR HOUSE DOESN'T APPRECIATE, WE'LL STILL BE FINE"

"You mean **if** it goes up, John," added Lucy. "Even in real estate, nothing is guaranteed. Of course, if our house doesn't appreciate, we'll still be fine, living in it and enjoying ourselves."

John laughed appreciatively. "That's my Lucy. Always the realist. **If** it goes up by $500,000. And **if** we ever sell our apartment building—which is already worth $250,000 more than what we paid for it—there's a way we can avoid paying any taxes on it as well."

He patted Lucy on the arm. "It's really something," he said. "I suppose we've been luckier than a lot of people. We certainly aren't the smartest folks around. But all in all, it really hasn't taken much effort for us to do as well as we have. Sometimes real estate seems so simple. We don't even manage the four-plex we own. Our real estate agent set us up with a property-management company that does it for us."

"And don't forget that first home of ours," Lucy pointed out. "We've been renting it to the same family for ten years. Sometimes I feel bad for them. I mean, with all the rent they've paid us over the years, they could have bought their own home. But they seem happy. Not everyone wants to own a home, I guess."

"AND NOW OUR KIDS ARE DOING IT, TOO"

As we were heading out of the coffee shop, buzzed from our lattes, I asked John and Lucy one last question: "Do you think what you did over the last 35 years can still be done today?"

John and Lucy looked at each other and smiled. "David," Lucy said, "it's being done every day. Most of our friends are like us."

John nodded. "Arizona is filled with people who are doing what we just did. You know, even our kids are doing it. It's funny, our biggest mistake—mine and Lucy's—was that we didn't get started until we were practically in our thirties. Thank goodness, neither of our daughters waited that long. Veronica is only 25 and she already owns a condo in San Diego that's doubled in three years. And her sister, Kathy, bought a home in Idaho that's gone up by 50 percent. They learned from us how it easy it can be. Now they're teaching their friends how to do it— and they are already getting ready to buy second homes."

THE MOST IMPORTANT THING IS HAVING THE RIGHT MINDSET

"John is right," Lucy said, "but there is one thing he's leaving out. The most important thing about what we did was having the right mindset. **We were people who thought poor for a long time.** We thought we would always be renters, and for ten years we were. But then one day, we expanded our thinking. We realized that we could actually go from renting to owning. And then, when we got to the point where we were ready to buy a bigger house, we realized that instead of selling our first house, we could keep it and become landlords. That changed everything."

She looked at me intently. **"Most people never change their mindset. If you do that, you can do what we did."**

I thought about what Lucy was saying. It sounded almost too easy to be true. "But what about discipline?" I asked. "I mean, it's one thing to decide to do something, but it's something else entirely to stick to that decision. Where did you get the discipline to put away the savings you needed and keep up with all those mortgage payments?"

"THE TRICK IS TO MAKE EVERYTHING AUTOMATIC"

John and Lucy burst out laughing. "Gosh," Lucy said, "we're probably the least disciplined people we know."

"The trick," John said, "is to make everything automatic. With the help of our bank, we automated everything from our savings programs to our mortgage payments. We even have our tenants deposit their rent payments automatically."

Lucy nodded thoughtfully. "It really is amazingly simple," she said, "I never imagined retirement could be so easy—or so much fun."

And with that I shook hands with John and Lucy, thanking them for the latte—and their story. Such nice people, I thought as I watched them walk down the street holding hands, such a simple plan.

They were, I realized, Automatic Millionaire Homeowners. Maybe someday I'd be one, too.

NOW IT'S YOUR TURN

The story of the Martins and how they got rich without a lot of effort or experience in real estate can become your story.

To find out how, turn the page and continue reading. You're about to enter the world of homeownership and real estate investing, a world that is far easier to understand—and to conquer—than you ever imagined. You are only a few hours away from a totally new way of thinking about where you live and how you live. If you're currently a renter, you will not want to continue doing that much longer, I promise you. And if you already own your home, you'll soon be thinking about buying another one—maybe several.

You are on your way to becoming an **Automatic Millionaire Homeowner.**

CHAPTER TWO

WHY SMART HOMEOWNERS FINISH RICH

Lucy Martin wasn't exaggerating when she said that the most important factor in becoming an Automatic Millionaire Homeowner is having the right mindset. Most people think becoming rich is a matter of luck or fate—that it's the kind of thing that happens to some people but never to them and that the best they can do is just plug along and try to keep their heads above water. Like Lucy said, they think poor.

But if there's any one lesson to learn from

the Martins' story, it's that **anyone can become rich**. And it's not nearly as hard as most people imagine. The fact is, there are simple strategies that don't require you to make a lot of money or to turn your life upside down in order to live and finish rich. And one of the simplest and most effective of all is becoming a homeowner.

So where do we begin?

Maybe not where you would think. You might think we should start by talking about how much home you can afford. That's where most books on real estate begin. But here's what I know from experience: It doesn't matter how much you can afford to spend on a home or a rental property if you don't have the confidence you need to buy one. Deciding to buy your first house (or your second when you haven't even paid off the first) can seem like a huge, scary thing to do—which may be why so many of us keep renting even though we know we probably shouldn't. Unfortunately, it's not always easy to find the confidence to overcome the fear.

This chapter is designed to give you that confidence. Once you have it, you'll be prepared to act. And it's actions—not good intentions—that change your life.

This chapter is only 34 pages long. You should be able to read it in less than 20 minutes. That's not very much time, but in it I'm going to share with you everything you need to know about real estate and why it's not too late for you to buy a home and get rich.

NOTHING BEATS HOMEOWNERSHIP AS A ROUTE TO RICHES

Of all the secrets to financial security I can share with you, nothing beats homeownership. Nothing. If you do it right— and that's not hard to do over time—you will ultimately make more money on your home than on any other investment you make. And, as I said before, if you buy a handful of homes over the course of your lifetime and rent them to other people, you won't just be financially secure, you'll be rich—maybe really rich!

This is exactly what happened to the Martins. It's what happened to me. It can happen to you.

As approaches to wealth go, homeowning is a rather boring one—but it works. And it allows you to sleep really well at night.

LISTEN TO THE SKEPTICS BUT KNOW THE FACTS

As I write this, the real estate skeptics are out in full force. They've been saying for five years now that the real estate boom is really just a bubble that is about to go bust. And in all fairness, they can cite some worrisome trends. One is the enormous amount of speculation currently taking place in "frothy" markets like Florida, San Diego, and Las Vegas, where increasing numbers of people are buying preconstruction condos not as residences but with the idea of "flipping" them for a quick profit. Another is the growing popularity of interest-only and adjustable-rate mortgages, both of which can lure unwary homebuyers into overextending themselves.

Given the enormous run-up in home prices, it would be surprising if speculators hadn't come swarming into the housing market. Everyone wants to make money fast. But if that's your goal, you've come to the wrong place. What we're talking about here isn't short-term speculation but long-term commitment. **This is a book about how to make solid decisions in real estate that will make you rich over a lifetime.**

I'm not promoting a "get rich quick" scheme here. I'm talking about a simple, timeless approach to living and finishing rich by investing in real estate.

How can I be so confident about the real estate road to riches? Well, the fact is that U.S. real estate values have been going up steadily for nearly four decades—an average of 6.3 percent a year since 1968, which is when the National Association of Realtors first started keeping track. According to Freddie Mac (a.k.a. the Federal Home Loan Mortgage Corporation), since 1950 U.S. house prices have **never** experienced a year-to-year decline nationally. Compare that to the S&P 500, a major stock-market indicator that has had no fewer than a dozen down years in the same period—or the market for U.S. Treasury bonds, which has fallen in 17 of the last 55 years.

If you still have doubts about whether owning real estate makes sense, here's something to think about: five factors that make homeownership a reliable road to wealth and four reasons why real estate is a good long-term bet. Spend the next ten minutes reading them. Then read them again.

When you're finished, you should understand why you need to own real estate. And then we'll jump into how you can go about getting some.

WHY OWNING REAL ESTATE CAN MAKE YOU RICH

HOMEOWNER FACTOR NO. 1: OWNING IS CHEAPER THAN RENTING

People who say it's cheaper to rent than to own are simply wrong. Under certain circumstances in certain markets (where real estate values are overheated and rents are low), there may be some short-term advantages to renting. But over the long haul, renting simply is not a good deal (except for the landlord whose mortgage you are paying).

If you don't own your own home, you can easily wind up spending more than half a million dollars on rent during the course of a lifetime—probably a lot more. Let's do the math. Say your rent is $1,500 a month. Over 30 years, that would add up to a total of $540,000 in monthly payments! But that's only if your rent never goes up—and whose rent stays the same for 30 years? Even with rent control, you're bound to have cost-of-living increases. And if you ever have to move—well, forget about it!

COMPARING RENTING TO HOMEOWNERSHIP—LOOK AT THE NUMBERS

Let's try to be at least a little realistic. Assume you're renting a house for $1,500 a month. Now let's say you stay put for 30 years, during which time the landlord increases the rent by 5 percent a year (which would be conservative). Over those 30 years, you will hand over to the landlord a total of nearly $1.2 million in rent payments—and at the end, you'll have nothing to show for it except a bunch of cancelled checks. To add insult to injury, you'll now be paying him $6,174 a month! How's that for depressing?

Now let's imagine that instead of continuing to rent, you've used the tools you'll learn in this book to buy the same home for $200,000. Initially, your costs as a homeowner, including mortgage payments, taxes, and maintenance, are likely to total around the same $1,500 a month that you would have paid in rent. But these costs won't balloon over the years the way rent would. That's because your regular mortgage payment, which represents the lion's share of your monthly outlay, is fixed (or, if you have an adjustable-rate mortgage, at least capped).

What will balloon over the years is the value of your house. Say it goes up by 6 percent a year, which is actually slightly lower than the national average. After 30 years, you will own a home that's worth just under $1.1 million. How amazing is that?

HOMEOWNER FACTOR NO. 2:
HOMEOWNERS GET LEVERAGE

What makes rich people really rich is leverage. Leverage is what you get when you use what is called "OPM," which stands for "other people's money." Buying properties with OPM gives you huge financial advantages, allowing you to multiply your gains. It's what you will use to buy real estate—the "other person" in this case being your bank or mortgage lender.

Here's how it works. Let's say you find a home you can buy for $200,000. Assuming the house really is worth that much, you shouldn't have too much trouble finding a bank to loan you at least 80 percent—or $160,000—of the purchase price. (As you will see in Chapter Five, you may even be able to get a bank to loan you 100 percent or more of the purchase price. But for now let's be conservative.)

This leaves you with a $40,000 down payment to make. You put up the cash, get a loan, and the house is yours.

Now let's say the value of the house goes up by 10 percent. So now it's worth $220,000, or $20,000 more than you originally paid for it.

If you were to sell the house at this point for $220,000, what kind of return do you think you would have just made? If your answer is 10 percent, you're mistaken.

Remember, you put down only $40,000 in cash. The bank put up the rest. But the bank doesn't share in your profits from a sale. They belong to you. The only thing due the bank is the repayment of the $160,000 you borrowed.

So you take the $220,000 that you got for the house and you repay the bank its $160,000 (minus the payments you've made to the principal so far). That leaves you with more than $60,000—or roughly $20,000

HOW LEVERAGE WORKS			
Assumes $40,000 down payment on a $200,000 house whose value increases by 6% a year			
	Value of House	Total Appreciation	Return on $40,000 Down Payment
AT START	$200,000	0	—
YEAR 1	$212,000	$12,000	30%
YEAR 2	$224,720	$24,720	62%
YEAR 3	$238,204	$38,203	96%
YEAR 4	$252,496	$52,495	131%
YEAR 5	$267,645	$67,645	169%
YEAR 6	$283,704	$83,704	209%
YEAR 7	$300,726	$100,726	252%
YEAR 8	$318,770	$118,770	297%
YEAR 9	$337,896	$137,896	345%
YEAR 10	$358,170	$158,170	395%

more than the $40,000 you originally put in. To put it another way, you made a $20,000 profit on a $40,000 investment—which amounts to a **50 percent return**.

But, remember, we were being conservative. As I write this, in hot markets like Miami, Las Vegas, and Phoenix, where real estate values have jumped more than 100 percent in the last five years, homebuyers have literally leveraged themselves into fortunes.

A great example of this is my friend Rick and his wife, Molly. Five years ago, they bought a house in Las Vegas for $200,000. At the time, the developer was offering a special loan program with a bank that required them to make a down payment of only 5 percent. So Rick and Molly put down $10,000. Actually, they didn't have $10,000 in cash. They borrowed $5,000 from their 401(k) plan at work and put $5,000 on their credit cards. Their friends told them they were crazy.

Not long ago, they sold their home. Are you ready for this? The sale price was $600,000!

After paying back their 401(k) loan and their credit cards, they pocketed nearly $400,000. Given that their initial investment was only $10,000, this amounts to a return of 4,000 percent in just five years!

As much as I like stocks, bonds, and mutual funds, there is little chance any of them will produce anything close to this kind of return. And there is no chance that anyone will lend you or me 80 percent or 90 percent or 100 percent of the purchase price to buy a stock, bond, or mutual fund. The same is true for gold, diamonds, artwork, stamps, limited partnerships—or whatever supposedly "sure thing" investment you can think of. Financial institutions simply won't lend people that kind of money to make these kinds of investments. When it comes to real estate, however, it's a different story. And the reason is simple—most people who buy a home will do anything to keep it. In fact, in any given year, banks wind up foreclosing on less than 1.5 percent of the home mortgages they make.

Home mortgages are such a good investment that many banks will often consider lending you 100 percent of the money you need to buy a home—and some will even make you hybrid loads of as much as 125 percent (25 percent more than the purchase price) if you have decent credit. Please note that I'm NOT recommending that you try to get yourself one of these loans. We'll cover the pros and cons of "no down payment" mortgages and all their variations later on. My point now is simply that it's a lot easier than you may think to buy a house with someone else's money—and then enjoy the benefits of the resulting leverage.

HOMEOWNER FACTOR NO. 3:
**HOMEOWNERS GET TAX BREAKS—
RENTERS DON'T**

The best way to stay poor is to pay more than you have to in taxes. As a renter, that's just what you're doing. **When you rent, you get absolutely zero tax breaks on your housing costs.** As a homeowner or real estate investor, you get a ton of them.

By far, the best—and best-known—tax

break that homeowners enjoy is the mortgage interest deduction. Very simply, when you own a home, the IRS allows you to deduct from your taxable income the interest charges you pay on the first $1 million of your home mortgage—which means that if your mortgage is $1 million or less, you get to deduct **all** your interest payments. (The limit rises to $1.1 million if you borrow $100,000 of it from a home equity line.) And since for the first ten years of a standard 30-year mortgage, nearly 80 percent of your monthly payment goes to pay off interest charges (as opposed to paying down the principal), in the early years at least, you can write off more than three-quarters of what you make in mortgage payments. (If you happen to have an interest-only mortgage— which we will cover later—you get to write off 100 percent of your monthly mortgage payment.)

Let's say you've got a $200,000 mortgage. As of this writing, mortgage rates are still around 6 percent, which means your monthly payment on a standard 30-year mortgage would be roughly $1,200. Since in the first year 83 percent of that $1,200 represents interest, you'd be able to write off just about $1,000—meaning that over the course of your first year of homeownership, you'd be able to take a tax deduction of nearly $12,000.

Assuming you're a typical taxpayer in the 30 percent bracket, that $12,000 deduction would reduce your tax bill by around $3,600. But a better way to think about it is that, at the beginning at least, your $1,200 monthly mortgage payment really costs you only about $900. In effect, the government is giving you a $300-a-month subsidy.

If you're a long-time renter and you have an accountant who hasn't explained this to you, you should find yourself a new accountant.

The point is that those tax deductions you get to take for mortgage interest are a GIFT from the government.

Take that gift!

> HOMEOWNER FACTOR NO. 4:
> **HOMEOWNERS CAN EARN**
> **TAX-FREE PROFITS**

Another way to stay poor (or at least middle-class) is to keep letting the government take part of the profits you make from your investments. Buy shares in Google at $300 and sell them at $600, and you've made a bunch of money, but not as much as you think. This kind of profit is called a capital gain, and as with virtually all income, the IRS insists on taking its cut. If your profit comes from the sale of a stock you held for 12 months or less, it's considered a short-term capital gain and you will pay ordinary income taxes on it. For most people, this means 30 percent of your profit will go to Uncle Sam. If you held the stock for more than 12 months, it's a long-term gain, and you get taxed at a lower but still hefty rate (from 5 percent to 15 percent, depending on your tax bracket).

There is one asset, however, that you can sell at a profit without having to pay capital gains taxes to the government. You guessed it—it's your home.

Remember my friends Rick and Molly, who bought a house for $200,000 and sold it five years later for $600,000? Well, they didn't have to pay one penny of their $400,000 profit to the government. That's right. Zero. Nada.

Here's why. Under current tax law, if you sell your primary residence (which the government defines as a place where you've lived for at least two years out of the last five), you don't have to pay any capital gains taxes on the first $250,000 in profits—the first $500,000 if you're married.

So, like Rick and Molly, if you're married, you can buy a home for $200,000 and sell it for $600,000 and earn $400,000 in tax-free income. Not only that, but you can then turn around and buy another home for $700,000, sell it later for $1.2 million, and pocket $500,000 in completely tax-free gains. And you can keep doing this, buying and selling and pocketing the profits tax-free, as many times as you like for as long as you want—or at least as long as the tax code stays the way it is.

If you happen to make more than $500,000 in profits on a sale (or more than $250,000 if you're single), it's no biggie. You simply pay capital-gains taxes on the amount by which you exceeded the cut-off.

DOWNSIZE TO THE RIGHT SIZE

A great way to take advantage of this terrific tax break is to do what's called "trading down." I like to think of this as "downsizing to the right size." Rick and Molly are following this strategy. They found a really nice house in a gated community outside of Las Vegas. The price was $350,000, so they used $70,000 of their $400,000 tax-free profit to make the 20 percent down payment. They're going to use the remaining $330,000 to buy two other homes that they are going to rent out. Because the tax-free sale left them with so much cash to put down, the mortgages on these rental properties should be very low—meaning they will be generating positive cash flow from the very start.

See how this can get to be fun?

> ### HOMEOWNER FACTOR NO. 5:
> ### HOMEOWNERS BECOME SAVERS

One of the most important features of homeownership—and the thing about it most responsible for making homeowners rich—is that owning a home turns you into a saver. Why is this important? It's simple. People who have money have it because they saved it. People who don't didn't.

Homeownership creates savers. Each time you make a mortgage payment, you're saving money. That's because with each payment you're reducing your loan balance a little—and that in turn is building you equity. (This assumes you don't have an interest-only loan.) The longer you own your home, the more equity you build, the more you save—and the richer you get.

WHY REAL ESTATE IS A GOOD LONG-TERM BET

By now you should have a good idea of the phenomenal financial advantages you get from owning versus renting. But change can be scary, and so can taking on big commitments like borrowing hundreds of thousands of dollars to buy a home. Lots of otherwise sensible people talk themselves out of becoming homeowners by convincing themselves that it's just too risky. But is that really true?

As I said earlier, this book is not about hype. So it's important to keep in mind that no investment—not stocks, not bonds, and not real estate—goes up in a straight line forever. Like most other asset values, real estate prices are cyclical. They go up and they go down. And when they go down, they can stay down for a long time. In the late 1980s, real estate prices tumbled in California and then stayed flat for nearly seven years. But in America over the long term (which is to say, ten years or more), there are many reasons why experts believe that homeownership is an exceptionally smart way to invest your money.

Here are the top four:

> LONG-TERM REASON NO. 1:
> **DEMOGRAPHIC CHANGE IS**
> **DRIVING DEMAND FOR HOUSING**

Say the word "demographics" and most people's eyes glaze over. But for homeowners, demographics couldn't be more thrilling. The fact is that demographic trends—including faster-than-predicted population growth, record immigration, and the aging of the "baby boom" generation—are combining in a way that guarantees demand for housing will stay strong for the foreseeable future. And continuing strong demand means prices are bound to keep rising.

Let's look at these trends individually.

- **THE U.S. POPULATION IS GROWING FASTER THAN PREDICTED**

According to a recent report by the Joint Center for Housing Studies at Harvard University, two unrelated trends—the tidal wave of immigration over the past 20 years and the fact that most Americans are living longer than ever—are combining to produce the highest level of net household growth the country has seen since the baby boom generation first entered the housing market in the 1970s. In fact, the Census Bureau predicts that between 2006 and 2015, the United States will add 2 million more households than the experts had previously thought.

As a result, there is not enough new housing currently on the drawing boards to meet the expected demand. While certain markets may currently be experiencing housing "booms" that could well lead to "gluts," most experts believe that on a national basis, we are looking at a long-term housing shortage.

- **RECENT IMMIGRANTS ARE BUYING
  MORE HOMES THAN EVER BEFORE**

As a result of the record number of foreign-born people who entered the United States over the past two decades, some 20 percent of all U.S. households are now headed by either an immigrant or the child of an immigrant. Once they've gotten a job and started sending money to their relatives back home, one of the first things immigrants do when they come to America is start saving to buy a home. Why? **Because owning a home is a key part of the American Dream—even for people who aren't yet Americans.**

- **RETIRING BABY BOOMERS WILL HAVE
  A HUGE IMPACT ON REAL ESTATE
  MARKETS**

It's not just immigration that's been responsible for the unprecedented run-up in real estate values over the last 30 years. As I just noted, the baby boom of the 1950s and early 1960s has also played a major role in stoking the huge continuing demand for housing. As the nation's 80 million baby boomers reach retirement age over the next decade or so, they will continue to impact real estate markets.

The amount of equity that baby boomers have in homes right now is staggering. And with the easy "cash-out refinancing" and home equity lines that so many banks are now providing, an increasing number of them are turning their equity into hard dollars that they are using to buy second and third "get-away" and vacation homes. Between 2002 and 2004, homeowners took a phenomenal $400 billion in cash out of their homes—and put a good deal of that money right back into real estate, purchasing a record 2.8 million second homes in 2004.

As a result, demand for housing has been soaring. And it's expected to continue doing so, particularly on the coasts, around resort communities, and in "second home" markets generally. This is yet another reason to be bullish about the long-term prospects for real estate values.

• THE ECHO GENERATION

Those 80 million baby boomers are leaving behind more than just a legacy of consumer demand. They've also had lots of children, record numbers of whom are now looking at real estate and buying homes at younger ages than ever before. Four main factors are helping to produce this "echo" effect in real estate markets: the proliferation of first-time homebuyer loan programs, record low interest rates, parents willing to help with down payments, and inheritances.

This last factor is especially significant. Between now and 2020, as the baby boom generation begins to pass, there is expected to be the largest intergenerational transfer of wealth the world has ever seen. This record-setting inheritance boom is going to make it possible for more young people to buy more homes than any generation before them.

LONG-TERM REASON NO. 2: IT'S EASIER TO GET FINANCING

The second reason real estate is such a good long-term bet has to do with changes in the way lenders handle financing. It used to be that homebuyers didn't have many choices when it came to financing. You could get a 30-year fixed mortgage or you could get a 15-year fixed mortgage. But then came the "creative financing" revolution. As a result, homebuyers today have literally hundreds of mortgage options to select from.

These days, you can choose between fixed, variable, or interest-only mortgages, with terms ranging from one year to 40 years. You can even get something called a negative amortization mortgage, with payments so small that over time your principal actually gets larger, rather than going down. These options emerged in an era of exceptionally low interest rates, but while the low rates may not last forever, it is likely that the new diversity of financing will.

The vast array of available mortgages is a

real boon to first-time homebuyers and experienced real estate investors alike, and
there is no doubt that the proliferation of
choices—and the increasingly easy access to
them—should keep the real estate market
humming for years to come.

> ### LONG-TERM REASON NO. 3:
> ### MORTGAGE COMPANIES NOW LEND
> ### TO RISKIER BORROWERS

This reason is really important because it
means that even if you have a bad credit
record or owe a lot on your credit cards, you
can still buy a home. To put it simply, the
banking industry is increasingly willing to
work with what are known as "sub-prime"
borrowers—people who have had credit
problems or simply have a hard time prov-
ing they are creditworthy. Reflecting this,
sub-prime mortgages went from being almost nonexistent in the 1990s to account-
ing for 10 percent of all mortgages in 2004.
My friends Jim and Rebecca are a great
example of this trend. Over dinner one
night in San Francisco, just before Rebecca

gave birth to their first child, they mentioned they were looking for a two-bedroom rental to replace the one-bedroom apartment they had been renting for the previous seven years. "Guys, I have a better idea," I said. "You should be buying a place. Continuing to rent is just crazy."

A little embarrassed, Jim confessed that there was a house they had their eye on, but their credit really wasn't the best—and they owed about $25,000 in credit card debt.

"No one is going to loan us a dime with our credit," moaned Rebecca.

I replied that you won't know until you ask.

Sure enough, the first lender they contacted turned them down, as did the second and the third. But they kept trying, and after three more rejections they found a bank that was willing to give them the no-money-down, $550,000 mortgage that they needed. Because their credit was bad, the interest rate was high—around 9 percent—but they got 100 percent financed. The mortgage even covered their closing and some minor fix-up costs.

Three years later, they sold their home for

more than $800,000. With the tax-free profits, they repaired their credit and paid off all their debts.

Increasing competition in the mortgage industry—and a growing realization among banks that lending to "sub-prime" borrowers like Jim and Rebecca isn't as risky as they used to think it was—means that more people who previously would have been shut out of the housing market will now be able to buy homes. The result will be more first-time homebuyers. And it's first-time homebuyers who ultimately drive the real estate market nationally.

> LONG-TERM REASON NO. 4:
> ## THE "1031" TAX BREAK FOR RENTAL PROPERTIES

While the capital-gains exemption that homeowners generally enjoy is a great deal, it does have one catch. You qualify for it only if you happen to be selling the house you actually live in. But that doesn't mean you have to share your profits with the government when you sell a rental property. You can cut out Uncle Sam by doing what's called a 1031 Exchange (1031 being the relevant section of the tax code).

Also known as a Starker Exchange (in honor of the real-estate investor T. J. Starker, whose challenge to the IRS led to the rule), rule 1031 says that when you sell a rental property, you don't have to pay any taxes on the profits as long as you use all the proceeds to buy another rental property within 180 days. Because of this, buying rental properties has become increasingly attractive to investors. Reflecting this, the dollar value of 1031 Exchanges has exploded, rising from $86 billion in 2001 to $210 billion in 2003. In 2004, San Francisco's Investment Property Exchange Services, one of the largest facilitators of 1031 Exchanges, saw its business increase by another 40 percent over 2003. For more details on how 1031 Exchanges work, visit **www.finishrich.com/ 1031exchange** to read and learn more on how to take advantage of this tax loophole.

NOW LET'S LOOK AT HOW YOU CAN GET STARTED

If you still have any doubts about becoming a first-time homeowner—or buying additional homes that you can rent out—go back and re-read this chapter. Between the equity you can build, the tax advantages you can enjoy, and the appreciation you can expect, it should be clear to you that homeownership is as close to a financial no-brainer as you can get.

Congratulations on reading this far. Now, it's time to start talking strategy—to learn how to find the money you'll need to buy your home or investment property.

It's going to be easier than you ever thought possible.

AUTOMATIC MILLIONAIRE HOMEOWNER ACTION STEPS

From here on out, each chapter will end with a series of **Automatic Millionaire Action Steps**. These steps are meant to summarize what you just read and motivate you to take immediate powerful action. Remember, inspiration unused is merely entertainment. To become an Automatic Millionaire Homeowner, you need to act on what you've learned.

Reviewing the actions we laid out in this chapter, here's what you should be doing right now to become an Automatic Millionaire Homeowner. Check off each step as you accomplish it.

❏ Adopt the Automatic Millionaire Homeowner Mindset and recognize that anyone can become rich—even you.

❏ Understand the difference between short-term speculation and long-term commitment—and which one really will make you rich.

❑ Decide right now you want to be an Automatic Millionaire Homeowner.

❑ Go to **www.finishrich.com/ homeowner/chaptertwo** to listen to the free audio supplement to this chapter.

CHAPTER THREE

THE AUTOMATIC DOWN PAYMENT SOLUTION

Now that you're ready to start building wealth through homeownership, it's time to talk "real world" about money—specifically, how much you're going to need to buy a house and where you're going to get it.

Given the steady run-up in prices over the years, it's easy to conclude that real estate has become a game for rich people only— that unless you've got piles of money lying around, you should forget about trying to play. In fact, nothing could be further from the truth. While having lots of hard cash in the bank can certainly make things easier, it's definitely not a necessity.

But before we get into the nitty-gritty of exactly how much—or, more accurately, how little—cash it takes to buy a home, there's an even bigger question we need to tackle.

HOW MUCH HOME CAN YOU AFFORD?

When it comes to investing in real estate, the bottom line isn't how much houses cost. It's how much you can afford to spend.

So how much home can you afford? There is no single answer to this important question—except maybe "more than you think."

And how much is that?

There are a number of ways to figure out how much you can afford to spend on a home. I think the most sensible rule of thumb is the one recommended by the Federal Housing Administration, the government agency charged with helping Americans become homeowners. It says that most people can afford to spend 29 percent of their gross income on housing (which is to say, mortgage payments, property taxes, and other regular costs)—and as much as 41 percent, if they have no debt. The following table should give you a good idea of the kind of price range your income would justify.

As the table on page 90 indicates, if you earn $50,000 a year, you should be able to afford to spend between $1,208 and $1,712 a month on housing, whether in the form of rent or mortgage payments. This may seem like a pretty wide range—and it is. Why? Because people earning the same income aren't necessarily in the same financial boat. Whether you should be on the high side or the low side of the FHA range is a judgment call that each of us must make individually, since it depends on a number of factors. These include how much debt you are al-

WHAT PRICE RANGE IS RIGHT FOR YOU?			
Annual Gross Income	Monthly Gross	29% of Gross	41% of Gross
$20,000	$1,667	$483	$683
$30,000	$2,500	$725	$1,025
$40,000	$3,333	$967	$1,367
$50,000	$4,176	$1,208	$1,712
$60,000	$5,000	$1,450	$2,050
$70,000	$5,833	$1,692	$2,391
$80,000	$6,667	$1,933	$2,733
$90,000	$7,500	$2,175	$3,075
$100,000	$8,333	$2,417	$3,417

ready carrying, what other financial goals or commitments you have (like retirement savings or special medical expenses), how secure your job is, and what your future prospects are. Obviously, if you have little or no debt, few other commitments, and are looking forward to a series of promotions at work, you can comfortably bump up against the 41 percent ceiling. If things are a little tight, you'll want to stay closer to the 29 percent floor.

TYPICAL MORTGAGE PAYMENTS

Monthly payments (principal and interest)
for 30-year, fixed-rate mortgage

Mortgage Amount	5.0%	5.5%	6.0%	6.5%	7.0%	7.5%	8.0%
$100,000	$537	$568	$600	$632	$668	$699	$734
$150,000	$805	$852	$899	$948	$998	$1,048	$1,100
$200,000	$1,074	$1,136	$1,199	$1,264	$1,331	$1,398	$1,468
$250,000	$1,342	$1,419	$1,499	$1,580	$1,663	$1,748	$1,834
$300,000	$1,610	$1,703	$1,799	$1,896	$1,996	$2,098	$2,201
$350,000	$1,879	$1,987	$2,098	$2,212	$2,329	$2,447	$2,568
$400,000	$2,147	$2,271	$2,398	$2,528	$2,661	$2,797	$2,935
$450,000	$2,415	$2,555	$2,698	$2,844	$2,994	$3,146	$3,302
$500,000	$2,684	$2,839	$2,998	$3,160	$3,327	$3,496	$3,665

And while confidence and optimism are absolutely essential to success, don't get carried away. Keep in mind that most of us have a tendency to view our financial situation in overly rosy terms. Above all, remember Murphy's Law—the time-tested adage that says, "If something can go wrong, it will"—and knock 10 percent to 20 percent off whatever your calculations say you can afford.

Keeping in mind that homeownership (buying) is better than home loanership (renting), check out the table on page 91. It shows what the monthly payments would be for different sizes of 30-year mortgages at different interest rates.

So what does this table tell us? Well, figuring an interest rate of around 5.75 percent (which, as I write this, is where standard 30-year fixed-rate mortgages are), what the table says is that someone who can afford to spend between $1,200 and $1,700 a month on housing—that is, someone who earns $50,000 a year—could easily carry a $200,000 to $300,000 mortgage. In most parts of the country, that's still more than enough to buy a pretty substantial home.

YOU DON'T NEED A BIG DOWN PAYMENT TO BUY

This is the most important truth there is about homebuying. It costs a lot less than you think. And I'm not just talking about mortgage payments. I'm also talking about the number-one misconception that keeps people from buying a home or rental property—the mistaken idea that they won't be able to afford the down payment. In fact, studies show that this "no down payment" syndrome is the number-one factor that keeps people from looking at homes or believing they can ever buy one.

It used to be true that if you didn't have a lot saved for a down payment—say, at least 20 percent of the purchase price—you would find it hard to get a mortgage. But things have changed . . . radically. As I said earlier, these days there are all sorts of programs sponsored by developers, lenders, and even the government that make it possible to buy a home with a down payment as small as just 5 percent or 3 percent of the purchase price—and in some cases with no down payment at all. We'll get into the details of these programs in Chapter Five. Right now, all you need to know is that you don't have to be rich to buy a home. You just have to **want** to be rich.

That's not to say you can (or should) buy a home if you're totally broke. Even if you manage to get a mortgage that covers 100 percent of the purchase price (meaning you don't have to make any down payment), you will still face what they call "closing costs"— fees for things like appraisals, inspections, title searches, and so on. These closing costs can easily run into the thousands of dollars. And while there are mortgages that cover both the purchase price and the closing costs, it's more than likely that you'll still need to have some money in the bank. Before they'll give you a mortgage, most lenders will want to see bank or brokerage statements indicating that you've saved up a financial cushion hefty enough to cover at least three months' worth of such basic homeownership costs as mortgage payments, taxes, utilities, and insurance premiums.

So even though you don't need to be rich to become a homeowner, you will need to have **some** money in the bank. With this in mind, let's look at how you can start immediately building up the funds you will need to get you on the road to becoming an **Automatic Millionaire Homeowner.**

SAVING FOR A HOME— AUTOMATICALLY

Remember John and Lucy Martin, my original Automatic Millionaire Homeowners? One of the things about their story that impressed me the most was how they used what had previously been their car payment money to fund what became their "home-buying account."

As you'll recall, John Martin had his

monthly car payment deducted from his paycheck. But once the car was paid off, the Martins didn't cancel the monthly deduction. Instead, they decided to redirect it to a credit union account they set up with the specific idea of saving for a home. It took them less than two years to reach their goal.

Setting up this homebuying account was their first step to homeownership—and to becoming Automatic Millionaire Homeowners. Now it's time for you to do the exact same thing. It's easy. Here's how.

OPEN YOUR "HOME SAVINGS ACCOUNT" AND GET STARTED

This doesn't need to be complicated. Today, as soon as you've finished reading this, make a date to go down to your local bank and open a savings account. Tell the bank you're not interested in an account that comes with an ATM card or checking privileges (because you don't want to be tempted to spend any of the money you put into it). Rather, you're looking for an account that offers the highest interest rate available. This may turn out to be what's called a money market account. A money market account is a mutual fund that invests your deposits in short-term government bonds. Although they are not always federally insured the way regular bank savings accounts are, money market accounts are safe and generally pay the highest rates, which makes them perfect for a homebuying account.

If you are starting with an initial deposit of less than $1,000, you may be quoted a very low interest rate. So shop around. Banks compete for customers like any other business, and there are plenty of them—both regular and online—that are willing to offer decent rates. And keep in mind that there are money market accounts that pay interest on balances of as little as $100.

NOW MAKE IT AUTOMATIC

There's no getting around it. In order for a savings plan to be effective, **the process has to be automatic.** Whatever you plan to do with the money you're saving—whether you intend to park it in a retirement account, stash it away as a security blanket, invest it in a college fund, or put it aside to help you buy a home—**you need to have a system that doesn't depend on you having to do anything.** This means setting up a regular payroll deduction or checking account transfer that automatically moves a specified amount of money to your savings account on a specific day of the month.

Having worked with clients as a financial advisor for many years, I can tell you that automatic plans are the only ones that really work. Clients would tell me all the time, "David, I'm super-disciplined. I'll put the money aside each month—I really will." They meant it. They believed it. But they were fooling themselves. Sticking to a savings plan is as hard as sticking to a diet—maybe harder. It's no accident that the U.S. savings rate dropped to near zero in 2005. We live in a consumer society that's constantly urging us not to save but to spend and buy.

So why torture yourself? Make the process

easy by making it automatic. This is exactly what the Martins did. Here's how you can do it.

> STEP ONE: **ARRANGE FOR YOUR PAYCHECK TO BE DEPOSITED AUTOMATICALLY IN YOUR BANK ACCOUNT**

The smartest thing you can do with your paycheck is have it deposited automatically into your bank account. This will save you both time and money! If you save yourself just a half hour every two weeks by not having to go to the bank to deposit your paycheck, you've just picked up thirteen extra hours a year. More important, you'll earn more interest on your money because it will be going into your account earlier.

Most employers offer direct deposit services, and most banks encourage it. All you need to do is provide your employer with the number of your checking account and wiring instructions for your bank (which the bank will be happy to give you).

STEP TWO: ARRANGE FOR AN AUTOMATIC FUNDS TRANSFER INTO YOUR HOME SAVINGS ACCOUNT

Since using direct deposit allows you to know exactly when your paycheck will be hitting your checking account, you can now pick a specific day (or days) of the month for a specific amount of money to be automatically transferred from your checking account to your Home Savings Account. If your paycheck gets deposited, say, on the 1st and 15th of each month, I would recommend that you have your bank make the transfer the very next business day (in this case, the 2nd and the 16th).

Virtually every bank offers this service—the technical term for it is **automatic funds transfer** or **systematic savings**—and it can all be arranged in a matter of minutes with a simple phone call or visit to your bank's web site.

MAKE IT EVEN EASIER BY DOING IT ONLINE

One way to make the process even easier— and to get some of the highest interest rates available—is to open your Home Savings Account online. As of this writing, two major online banks—**Emigrant Direct** and **ING Direct**—are aggressively pursuing new customers with high interest rate accounts that don't require you to maintain a minimum balance. (You can contact Emigrant Direct online at **www.emigrantdirect.com** or by phone at 800-836-1997. ING Direct is reachable online at **www.ingdirect.com** or by phone at 800-ING-Direct.) As I write this in the summer of 2005, the rates on these high-yield savings accounts are five times the national average. While many banks are offering 1 percent on their savings accounts, these online banks are offering upward of 4 percent. And in some cases, the accounts offered by these online banks are now also FDIC-insured. Their only disadvantage is that they are not "brick and mortar" banks—meaning you can't walk into a branch and meet with a real person face to face. Still, if you have questions, you can pick up the phone and call them. And you can open your Home Savings Account online in just minutes, without ever leaving home.

You can find the most up-to-date list of deals on banks and rates online at **www. bankrate.com** and **www.lowermybills.com.**

MAYBE YOUR REGULAR BANK CAN DO BETTER

The amazing rates offered by aggressive on-line banks have forced "regular" banks to take notice. As a result, many national banks now offer comparable high-yield savings accounts of their own. So before you switch, ask your regular bank, "Do you have a rate that competes?" You may find the answer is "yes"—in which case you won't have to change banks. And in some cases, the high-yield savings accounts offered by national banks are even FDIC-insured.

HOW MUCH SHOULD I SAVE?

Once you've got your Home Savings Account set up, how much should you transfer from your paycheck every two weeks? Obviously, that depends on your particular circumstances. But remember—saving up the money you'll need to become a homeowner should be your top financial priority.

SPEEDING UP THE PROCESS: SIX SHORTCUTS TO HOMEOWNERSHIP

Even with automatic transfers, the process of saving enough money to cover even a small down payment **plus** closing costs **plus** a financial cushion can still take months or years. If that seems too long to wait, you might consider one of these six shortcuts to homeownership.

SHORTCUT NO. 1:
**BORROW THE DOWN PAYMENT
FROM THE BANK**

As I mentioned earlier, it is not only possible but actually relatively easy to buy a home without having to come up with the cash for a down payment. In addition to 100 percent mortgages, which cover the entire purchase price, there are also what are known as 90/10 loans, in which you get a first mortgage that covers 90 percent of the purchase price and then a second mortgage that covers the down payment. (I'll discuss the details—along with the pros and cons— of these kinds of loans in Chapter Five.) You'll still need to have some cash in the bank before you can buy, but putting aside enough money for closing costs and that three-month financial cushion won't take as long as saving up for a 10 percent to 20 percent down payment.

> ### SHORTCUT NO. 2:
> ### BORROW THE DOWN PAYMENT
> ### FROM A RELATIVE

One result of the huge increase in real estate values is that there are more and more parents and grandparents who, because of the homeowners' equity they've built up over the years, are in a position to help their kids buy a home of their own. Don't misunderstand me: I'm not necessarily suggesting that this is something your parents or grandparents should do. (So, parents and grandparents, please don't blame me if you get asked!) As a rule, I discourage lending money to family members. That's because most such "loans" wind up becoming gifts. But there is an exception to every rule, and I know from my experience as a financial advisor that if there is one kind of "family loan" that makes sense, it's when parents lend their kids the money they need to make a down payment on a home. The parents feel great about it, the kids are grateful—and in most cases the loan is eventually paid back.

If you approach your parents or grand-parents for such a loan, you should present your request as an investment opportunity—not a handout. Certainly, you should offer to pay them interest on the money you borrow. Indeed, if the going interest rate on a five-year bank certificate of deposit is 5 percent, why not offer them 6 percent or 7 percent?

If you think you're going to be in the home a relatively short period of time, you can structure the loan so that you don't have to pay it back until you sell the property. Alternatively, you can structure it to allow you to repay it "as soon as possible"—so if the property appreciates in value, you can refinance and pay off the loan with the proceeds.

SHORTCUT NO. 3:
BORROW THE DOWN PAYMENT
FROM YOUR RETIREMENT ACCOUNT

Another potential source of funds for a down payment may be your retirement plan.

If you've been contributing to a 401(k) plan at work, you may be able to borrow up to $50,000 from your account. It depends on the nature of your company's plan—**and you need to be very careful**—but under the right circumstances, this can be a very simple thing to do.

Here's how it works. Most 401(k) plans have provisions that allow you to borrow from your account. Check with the benefits department at work to see if this is true of yours. If it is, they will send you the necessary forms to fill out. Among other things, you will be asked what you are borrowing the money for. Once you explain it's to buy a home, your request should be quickly approved.

The catch here is that even though it's all your money, it really **is** a loan—meaning you have to pay interest on it and you have to pay it all back. Of course, all the interest and principal you pay go to your retirement account—which is to say, back to you. But there are disadvantages. For one thing, you have to start repaying your 401(k) loan right away. For another, during the time your money is on loan, it is not compounding in your account—meaning you're losing the benefit of years of investment gains. So this shouldn't be your first choice for a down-payment solution. Still, it is an option well worth considering.

Please study the risks listed below carefully because there are some big ones. And if you choose this option, make it automatic! Set up an automatic funds transfer to take care of the repayments you'll have to make to your 401(k) account.

A WARNING ABOUT BORROWING FROM YOUR RETIREMENT ACCOUNT

The warning about this really being a loan is no minor detail. If you don't repay all the principal, or if you fail to pay interest on it, the IRS won't consider it a loan but rather an early withdrawal—and that can cost you a bunch of money. That's because if you take money out of a 401(k) plan before you reach the age of 59½, the withdrawal is considered income on which you must pay income taxes. On top of that, you'll be assessed a 10 percent penalty. So if you borrow $20,000 from your retirement account but fail to do it correctly, you could easily wind up owing the IRS $10,000 in taxes and penalties.

You should also keep in mind that a loan from a 401(k) plan usually has to be repaid within five to ten years. It depends on how your 401(k) plan is set up—so be sure to ask. And DON'T do this if there's a chance you may be leaving your job in the near future. Your employer may require you to pay back the loan when you leave the company. **Check out if these conditions apply before you take the loan.**

> SHORTCUT NO. 4:
> **TAKE ADVANTAGE OF THE**
> **"HOMEBUYER'S LOOPHOLE"**

There are some exceptions to the rules that penalize you for taking money out of a retirement account too early. One of these loopholes is for first-time homebuyers, who are allowed to withdraw up to $10,000 from an IRA for a home purchase without having to pay the 10 percent penalty. You still have to pay income tax on the money (unless, of course, it's coming from a Roth IRA, the proceeds of which are always tax-free). So if you took out $10,000, you might have to pay $3,000 of it to Uncle Sam at the end of the year.

One of the nice things about this loophole is that the government defines a first-time homebuyer simply as someone who hasn't purchased a home within the last two years. So even if you already own a home, as long as you bought it more than two years ago, you can qualify for this exception. And you can do it again two years from now.

SHORTCUT NO. 5:
MAKE A RADICAL LIFE CHANGE

What keeps many renters from buying a home—or homeowners from investing in a rental property—is that they're not willing to change their current lifestyle in order to get what they really want. Every day, I meet people who live in great apartments, lease great cars, and wear wonderful clothes. But they tell me they can't save for the home they want because they are living paycheck to paycheck!

My response is always the same: "Well, how about downsizing your lifestyle a little? Move into a smaller apartment. Live in a less fashionable neighborhood. Drive a less expensive car. Buy fewer clothes. Eat out a little less. Make some changes."

More often than not, they'll shrug and say, "You're right—I **should** do that." And then a year later, I'll run into them and find they're still renting.

Fortunately, there are also exceptions to the rule, people who take charge of their lives and make things happen!

SIX MONTHS OF SACRIFICE—A
LIFETIME OF FINANCIAL FREEDOM

My friend George is a great example of this. When he and his wife, Donna, first got married, they were renting an apartment in San Francisco. They really wanted to buy a home, but no matter how hard they tried, they couldn't seem to save enough.

After complaining for a while about the incredibly high price of housing in the Bay Area, they did something life-changing. In order to be able to save what they needed for a down payment, they moved in with Donna's father for six months.

They'd just had their first child, and I remember George saying to me, "David, I don't know if we'll be able to make this work. I mean, Donna's dad is amazing, and we're really lucky that he offered to put us up. But can you imagine being married with a kid and living with your parents to save money?"

As it turned out, George and Donna survived living with Donna's dad just fine. In fact, it was great for everyone. Donna's dad got to spend time with his grandson—and Donna and George were able to save every dime they earned for six months. They used the money to put a down payment on a little house in an area that was not yet booming. The place needed work, and it was about thirty minutes farther out than they wanted to live, but it cost them only $225,000.

That was six years ago. Today, the house is worth more than $750,000! Just last year, George and Donna refinanced the place and pulled some money out so that George could realize his longtime goal of running his own business. He and Donna are now living their dreams—all because they were willing to make just a six-month change in their lifestyle.

What kind of lifestyle change could you make right now to have the future you want?

> ### SHORTCUT NO. 6:
> ### FIND YOUR LATTE FACTOR® AND
> ### DOUBLE LATTE FACTOR™

There wasn't any way I could write this book and not slip this in. If you've read any of my other books, seen me on television, heard me on the radio, or come across my philosophies in a newspaper or magazine interview, you know the Latte Factor is my "mantra." It's my metaphor for how we all spend lots of money on little things—and how we can save ourselves a fortune (maybe a down payment) if we just start keeping track of where it goes and holding on to some of it.

This idea has changed so many people's lives that it's worth repeating. And if you haven't heard of the Latte Factor or Double Latte Factor, you need to. So here goes.

USING THE LATTE FACTOR TO FIND THE MONEY FOR A DOWN PAYMENT

We've all got more money than we think. The problem is that we often waste it on small things that we want but don't really need.

The fastest way to save money for a home (or anything else, for that matter) is for you to figure out where all your hard-earned money is going—and then learn to hang on to it rather than spend it. This is the essence of the Latte Factor. For example, say you go to Starbucks every morning and get a grande nonfat latte. Right there, you're looking at about four bucks! Add a nonfat muffin to that and you've spent closer to $7!

Drop $7 dollars a day on a latte and a nonfat muffin, and you're spending $210 a month on coffee and muffins. That's about $2,500 a year. Hmm—where else in your life are you wasting money like this? Maybe it's not on lattes. And don't get me wrong— I'm not picking on coffee. I happen to like a good latte from Starbucks every once in a while myself. **As I said, the Latte Factor is a metaphor.**

Could your weakness be bottled water? Bottled water is a $10 billion-a-year industry in North America. How much of that came out of your pocket this month? Maybe it's cigarettes. You can easily spend $300 a month on cigarettes. If you rent and you smoke—stop smoking! You'll be able to become a homeowner in only a few years, and you'll live longer. Seriously.

If you're looking for a fast way to save

for a home, the bottom line is that it's all about the small stuff. Finding your Latte Factor can really help you see that you're already earning enough to be able to save for a home. Your problem is just that you're spending too much of it. Change your habits for twelve months, and before you know it, you'll have what you need to buy a home.

THE DOUBLE LATTE FACTOR—THE FASTEST WAY TO FIND THE MONEY

The Double Latte Factor (a concept I introduced in my last book, **Start Late, Finish Rich**) is something you use when you really want to make the most of what you earn. The idea here is that you take a hard look at your fixed overhead (that is, your regular monthly costs) and then cut them back a little.

A great example is cable TV service. Let's say you've got a typical deluxe cable package and you're spending $80 a month on 200 channels, 190 of which you never watch. I'm

TAKE THE DOUBLE LATTE FACTOR CHALLENGE—AND WIN A FREE LATTE MUG

You can win a free Latte Factor mug (perfect for drinking your home-brewed coffee) by sharing your Latte or Double Latte Factor experience in an e-mail to me at success@finishrich.com. Just tell me what happened to you when you took the challenge. How much money did you find? What did you learn? We'll select a new winner every day!

Since making similar offers in **The Automatic Millionaire** and **Start Late, Finish Rich,** I've received thousands of success stories from readers around the world. It's a simple idea that is really working. I urge you to visit my web site at **www.finishrich.com** and read how the Latte Factor is changing the lives of people just like you. Maybe their stories will inspire you. Maybe your story will wind up inspiring someone else!

THE DOUBLE LATTE FACTOR CHALLENGE

Calculating your Double Latte Factor means looking not just at your daily expenses, but at your weekly, monthly, seasonal, and annual expenses to find items and services big and small that can be eliminated or reduced for big savings.

Name: _____   Day: _____   Date: _____

	Item or Service	Cost	Wasted Money?		Amount Saved	Amount Saved Monthly
	What I bought or buy	How much I spent or spend	✓ if this can be eliminated	✓ if this can be reduced	I can save X amount by doing Y!	
Item Example	Bagel with cream cheese and small coffee	$3.50		✓	$2 per day by eating at home	$60
Service Example	Two cell phones for myself and Michelle	$200/mo. including all extra fees		✓	$50/mo. by changing service plans	$50
1						
2						
3						
4						

5					
6					
7					
8					
9					
10					
11					
12					
13					
14					
15					
My Double Latte Factor (Total Amount I Can Save Monthly) $					

not suggesting you give up your television. Just cut back to basic cable service and knock your monthly bill down to $29. That alone would save you an additional $600 a year that you could put toward a down payment on a house.

Then there's your phone bill. Do you really need both a regular home phone **and** a cell phone? If you let your home phone go, you could probably save another $500 a year! And that cell phone bill—do you really use 1,000 minutes a month? Couldn't you save another $30 a month by reducing the minutes and not going over each month? That could help you save another $400 a year.

The Latte Factor and the Double Latte Factor are designed to help you focus on precisely how you spend money. Remember, the faster you can figure out where your money is going, the faster you will be able to save. And the faster you can save, the faster you will achieve your dream of becoming an Automatic Millionaire Homeowner.

So with this in mind, go find your Latte

Factor! Use the form on page 118 to figure out where your money is going—and then start channeling more of it into your Home Savings Account.

HOW DO I KNOW WHEN I'M DONE?

Once you've found your Latte Factor and your Double Latte Factor, and you've programmed your automatic deposits to transfer as much as you can every time you get paid—and once you've added in your bonuses, birthday checks, garage-sale proceeds, tax refunds, and office-pool winnings (you name it)—how do you know when you've saved enough? My advice is to save for a year or two and then buy as much house as you can afford with the down payment and cushion that you have amassed. Many people make the mistake of waiting for years to save enough to make a down payment on their "dream house"—with the result that they never get into a home at all.

Remember what the Martins said—buying your dream home begins with the purchase of your first home.

Remember, your time in the market is money—so don't waste time and don't waste money. Go shopping for your home sooner rather than later.

NOW THE FUN BEGINS—LET'S GO FIND YOU A MORTGAGE

You now know how to save automatically for a down payment and closing costs on the purchase of a home. You've looked at some short cuts to the savings game, and you're working on finding extra money with the Latte Factor.

Now it's time to learn about the billions of dollars that are out there waiting for you to borrow so you can buy a home or rental property. The mortgage market is currently as exciting as it is confusing. But what really matters is that the huge number of financing options available these days makes homebuying easier than ever before.

So let's find out where and how you can get the money it will take to make that homebuying dream of yours real.

AUTOMATIC MILLIONAIRE HOMEOWNER ACTION STEPS

Reviewing the actions we laid out in this chapter, here's what you should be doing right now to start saving for a down payment—automatically.

❏ Using the tables on pages 90 and 91, and adjusting for your particular circumstances, figure out what price house you should be considering.

❏ Arrange to have your paycheck automatically deposited directly into your bank account.

❏ Open a Home Savings Account and arrange to fund it with an automatic transfer from your regular bank account.

❏ Speed up the savings process by finding your Latte Factor and using the other shortcuts to homeownership.

❏ Visit **www.finishrich.com** and read the Latte Factor Success stories—then run your own numbers at the Latte Factor calculator in the resource area of the web site. (And if you have a success story, share it with us!)

❏ Go to **www.finishrich.com/ homeowner/chapterthree** to listen to the free audio supplement to this chapter.

CHAPTER FOUR

HOW TO FIND A MORTGAGE ADVISOR YOU CAN TRUST

OK, so you're ready to buy a home.

Well, not quite. One of the most important things I can tell you about becoming an Automatic Millionaire Homeowner is before you start shopping for a home, you should shop for your mortgage.

You need to find the money first! After all, you may have all the confidence in the world that you can afford to carry a mortgage of a certain size, but if the bank isn't willing to lend you that much money, you're not going to get very far in the marketplace. And the truth is that until you meet with a mortgage professional and have him or her evaluate your situation, there's no way of knowing for sure how far the banks will be willing to go with you.

When you meet with a mortgage banker or broker—which is what you do when you go shopping for financing—you will find out exactly how much you're going to be able to borrow and how much that borrowing is going to cost you. Knowing all this in advance is not only smart—it's the only sensible way to proceed. It will save you time, effort, and possibly heartache when you actually start looking at real estate. And most important, if you are worried about being caught in a real estate bubble, the best thing you can do to "bubble-proof" your purchase is get the financing right.

Remember, it's not enough to be able to afford your home—**you ultimately have to be able to afford your mortgage!**

GETTING PAST THE FEAR

For most of us, buying a home is the biggest financial decision we'll ever make. Even if it's not the first time you've done it—even if you've bought two, three, or more homes in your lifetime—it's still a huge, huge step. And big steps can be scary.

So how do you get over the fear? Well, one way is to educate yourself so you can be sure of doing the right thing. **This is what you're doing right now.** The fact is that what you are learning in this book will make you smarter about buying a home and getting a mortgage than 95 percent of the people out there. And you can build on what you learn here by getting yourself some expert advice from a professional who can help you evaluate the many options available to you.

Everybody's circumstances are different. I can be your coach and guide, offering you encouragement and explaining to you the ins and outs of what can often be a complicated and confusing landscape. But without knowing the details of your situation, I can't tell you that one particular kind of mortgage product makes more sense for you than another. A good mortgage advisor, **who knows you and your finances**, can.

In this chapter, I'll show you first how to find one—and then how to work with him or her to make sure you get the best deal you can on a mortgage.

MORTGAGE ADVISORS— WHO THEY ARE AND WHAT THEY DO

There are two basic types of mortgage advisors. The first type is what is known as a "direct lender." Also referred to as a mortgage banker or consultant, they often work at a bank or other lending institution. Being a direct lender means that they are licensed to give funds directly to the customer.

The second type of mortgage advisor is a mortgage broker. Mortgage brokers don't actually lend money themselves. Instead, they put you together with banks and other institutions that do, and they work with you to get your loan approved.

What mortgage bankers and brokers have in common is that both are sales people. Both earn their livings by putting mortgage customers (you) together with mortgage providers (the banks and other lending institutions that pay them). So they definitely have a financial incentive to sell you on something. The good ones, however, know that no one benefits when a consumer is persuaded to take a mortgage that's not right for him or her. **The question, then, is how to find a good one.**

DIRECT LENDERS VS. MORTGAGE BROKERS

The next time you're in your local bank, mention to one of the tellers that you're interested in a home mortgage. In most cases you'll be escorted to a desk in the front of the bank and introduced to a nice man or woman with a title like "mortgage coun-selor," "homebuying coach," or something similarly friendly. This person is typically a mortgage banker. Their job is to assist you in the process of applying for a mortgage. They will review your financial situation as well as your needs and goals and walk you through the process of obtaining a mort-gage. Ask this person, "Are you a mortgage banker or a mortgage broker?" Knowing which they are will help you better under-stand how they work.

When you work with a mortgage banker, you are working with a direct lender. There are a number of advantages to doing this. For one thing, their conduct and business practices are tightly regulated by the government. For another, if the lender hap-pens to be a bank and you already have an account with them, they may offer you a "good customer" discount on your mortgage rate that could save you thousands of dollars in interest over the life of your loan. Also na-tional banks often "service" their own loans (that is, handle the monthly billing) themselves, rather than outsourcing it to some company you've never heard of. They do this because they want to make sure that you're well taken care of, so you'll come back to them the next time you need a loan.

Working with a direct lender can also be an advantage when it's time to refinance. (Refinancing means paying off your current mortgage by taking out a new mortgage.) Because they are already familiar with you and your house, you can often refinance in minutes with reduced fees. I once refinanced my home with my bank while lying by a pool in Hawaii. The whole process took ten minutes and saved me thousands of dollars.

Finally, if you are looking to buy your first home, it may help to work with a direct lender because most specialize in helping first-time homebuyers, and they may offer special programs that can make it easier for you to get your mortgage.

A mortgage broker, by contrast, doesn't work for a single bank. They are typically independent consultants, though they may work for a large national company. **The key**

difference with a mortgage broker over a banker is that they can shop your loan to various lenders. Unlike a mortgage banker, who represents his or her company, a mortgage broker doesn't represent any one lender. So in addition to reviewing your financial situation, they will look at mortgage products from more than one company. They often refer to this as "shopping" your loan for the best deal.

Common sense would tell you that a mortgage broker who shops your loan request to many sources should be able to get you a better deal than a mortgage banker, who is tied to just one institution. However, this is not always the case. As I noted earlier, if you are a customer of a national bank, you might be able to get a better deal there than where a mortgage broker would place you. This is because many banks offer discounts to regular customers. That said, banks also get a lot of business from mortgage brokers, and to keep the business coming, they offer special deals to them as well.

The main advantage to using a mortgage broker is often specialization. There are mortgage brokers who specialize in the luxury market or loans for self-employed people or a particular loan product that a mortgage banker might not be familiar with.

HOW YOUR BANKER OR BROKER GETS PAID

Whether you wind up selecting a mortgage banker or a mortgage broker, neither of them is going to work with you for free. And of course you wouldn't expect them to. The fact is, they often wind up spending hours going over your finances, organizing your loan documents, and walking you through the complicated, time-consuming process of getting your mortgage. They will keep track of the paperwork and try to keep you calm (which is not a small thing if you are buying your first home or investment property).

Both mortgage bankers and mortgage brokers are usually paid a commission on the loans they close. Who pays the commission? As a rule, it's you, the borrower—

though you may not always realize it, since the cost of the commission is generally amortized in the cost of the loan.

POINTS OR NO POINTS— YOU CHOOSE

In some cases, you will be told that if you are approved for a mortgage, you will have to pay a certain number of "points" up front. (A point is 1 percent of the total amount you're borrowing; two points on a $500,000 mortgage, for example, equals $10,000.) These points are the fee you pay for all the work the banker or broker has done to secure you your mortgage.

Sometimes there aren't any points. "No-points" mortgages are increasingly popular, and these days most borrowers prefer them. I've personally never paid a single point on a loan. But that doesn't mean I got my loans for free. In no-point loans, the commission is typically "wrapped into" the loan in the form of a slightly higher interest rate. Say the banker or broker offers you a 30-year mortgage at 6 percent. It's entirely possible they may actually be getting the mortgage at an interest rate of 5.5 percent, charging you a half percent more and pocketing the difference. This is called a yield-spread premium—**and it's totally legal.**

In most cases, the mortgage advisor won't volunteer what the "yield-spread" premium is. Still, it never hurts to ask your advisor how he or she is being compensated. My suggestion is to avoid "points" if you can, unless you plan to keep the property for a very long time (say, more than ten years) and you want to lower your interest rate. When you pay additional points (called "discount points"), you absorb the commission up front and prepay some of your interest.

FINDING A MORTGAGE ADVISOR YOU CAN TRUST

Not all advisors are the same. You want to work with a really top-notch professional whom you can trust.

So how do you find one? The best financial

people I know all give the same advice: Ask for a recommendation from a friend in the business, a real estate agent, an attorney, or someone you know who recently had a good experience getting a mortgage.

Well, that's fine if you know someone like that. But what if you don't?

Here's what I recommend. If you already bank with a national bank (or even a local one), start there. Go into the bank and ask to meet with a loan specialist. Have them review your situation, and see what they can offer you. Ask them if based on your existing "banking relationship" with them, you qualify for any preferred rates. This may sound silly if you have a really small bank account, but you can never tell what they may offer unless you ask! And the answer may be a resounding "Yes!"

Then, to make sure your bank is really doing the best it can for you, talk to a few mortgage companies. How do you find one? It's as simple as looking in your local paper in the real estate section. Read the ads: See who's offering what (including the national banks). Look at the advertisements and see whose pitch seems aimed at someone like you. For example, some companies make a point of emphasizing that they welcome first-time homebuyers, while others say they specialize in jumbo loans (at this printing, loans greater than the government-determined maximum of $359,650).

Once you have identified a mortgage advisor who seems appropriate, call him or her and make an appointment to go in and discuss your situation.

Following is a list of questions to ask the mortgage advisors you meet with. I'd also ask these questions of an advisor who has been recommended by a friend.

It shouldn't take you much more than ten minutes to go through the list—and believe me, it will be worth the effort. Keep in mind that selecting a mortgage can be the biggest financial decision you ever make. Shaving just 1 percent off your interest rate on a $200,000 mortgage will save you nearly $50,000 over the life of the loan! So take the time to choose the best advisor you can find.

FIVE QUESTIONS THAT WILL HELP YOU CHOOSE A GREAT MORTGAGE ADVISOR

QUESTION NO. 1:
HOW LONG HAVE YOU BEEN IN THE BUSINESS?

It's important to know how much experience your mortgage advisor has. Selecting a mortgage is too important a decision for you to be willing to work with a rookie (sorry to those brand new in the business). Your mortgage advisor should have a minimum of three years experience and, ideally, more. In addition, ask them how many loans they arranged last year and what type of mortgage products they tend to recommend and why. Make sure to ask if the mortgages they handled were for new purchases or refinancings. If you are looking to buy your first home and the advisor's experience is mainly with refinancings, he or she may not be the right one for you. A solid mortgage advisor should have arranged at least 24 purchase mortgages in the previous year; the higher the number, the better.

> QUESTION NO. 2:
> **WHAT IS YOUR PROCESS FOR GETTING ME A MORTGAGE?**

Applying for a mortgage is a lot like applying to college. There are all kinds of application forms to fill out, scores to worry about, and choices to make. Above all, it's important to make sure your expectations are in line with your abilities. Ask the banker or broker to spell out the process he or she will go through to help you do all these things. You should also ask them whether they will help you get "pre-approved" for a mortgage (a real commitment to lend you money), how long it is likely to take, and whether a fee is involved. I'll explain more about this crucial step shortly, but for now you should know that if the answer is, "No, but I can get you pre-qualified" (not a real commitment), this is not a broker or banker you want to work with.

QUESTION NO. 3:
WHAT KIND OF LOANS
DO YOU RECOMMEND?

Good advisors will tell you they recommend loans based on the client's particular needs and situation. Of course, there are some who say this and then offer the same kind of mortgage to everyone. So ask which kinds of mortgages your potential advisor favors and why. If you're not comfortable with their explanations, or if you can't understand them, find someone else.

QUESTION NO. 4:
DO YOU SPECIALIZE IN A CERTAIN
KIND OF CLIENT OR PRODUCT?

Some mortgage professionals welcome first-time homebuyers. Others work mainly with sophisticated investors. The key is to find a mortgage specialist who works with the type of borrower you happen to be. What's more, the size and type of loan he or she tends to do should be consistent with the kind of mortgage you're looking for. Obviously, if

you have limited funds and intend to purchase a modest home, you don't want to
hook up with an adviser who specializes in
high-end clients looking to finance multimillion-dollar mansions. Similarly, if you're
interested in a low-down-payment or interest-
only mortgage, you want a banker or broker with demonstrated know-how in this
area.

> QUESTION NO. 5:
>
> **CAN I COUNT ON GOOD SERVICE
> BOTH BEFORE AND AFTER
> I GET MY MORTGAGE?**

There are really two phases to the mortgage
process: before you get your loan and after-
ward. You want to be well taken care of during both of them. Here's how you can ensure
you will.

THE "BEFORE" PHASE

Getting approved for a mortgage and "closing" on the purchase of a home is a process
that usually takes weeks (and can sometimes

take months) to complete. During this time you will want to be in regular touch with your mortgage advisor and/or lender.

Here is what you should ask a potential mortgage broker or banker to determine if you will be treated properly while you're waiting to be approved:

- How often will you contact me during the approval process?
- How can I get in touch with you if I need information? (A good advisor encourages contact whenever the borrower feels it's necessary and should provide complete contact information, including telephone numbers, e-mail addresses, and pager information.)
- If you are not available, whom else can I call for help or assistance?
- Does your company conduct customer satisfaction surveys? What are their results? What are YOUR results as an advisor? (A company that

cares about its customers tracks this data—and often publishes it.)

THE "AFTER" PHASE

Once you close on your mortgage, you're not just getting a loan. You're beginning a relationship that could last for years.

Here is what you should ask a potential lender to determine if you will be treated properly after you've gotten your mortgage and closed on your house.

- Will you be servicing my mortgage after it closes, or will you be selling the servicing to another company? (Generally speaking, you get the best service from lenders who continue to service their mortgages after closing. That's certainly been my experience.)
- Are your monthly statements easy to read? Can you provide me with a sample statement?

- Can I access my mortgage statements online?
- Do you have a mortgage statement voice response unit (that is, an automated telephone voicemail system that you can call to find out your current balance)?
- Can I make extra payments on my principal? Will my statement clearly show how extra payments have been applied to my mortgage?
- If there's a problem with my mortgage, whom do I call for help?
- What happens if I'm late on my mortgage payments? Are there penalties?
- What happens if I have a long-term financial issue (such as job loss, chronic medical problem, or natural disaster) that prevents me from making my mortgage payments?
- Do you stay in touch regarding refinancing options? Will you proactively look for ways to save me money on my mortgage should rates

go down? (A smart lender will have a systematic way to stay in touch so he can do more business with you.)

IF YOU'RE NOT COMFORTABLE, KEEP ON LOOKING

The answers you get to these questions should give you a sense of whether the mortgage professional you're talking to is the right advisor for you. Chemistry should count for something, too. You're going to be discussing a lot of sensitive personal information with your mortgage advisor, so if you don't feel comfortable with him or her, the relationship is not going to work.

And don't settle for the lesser of two evils. If neither of the professionals you meet with seems to be the right fit, thank them for their time and keep on looking.

IT'S TIME TO GO SHOPPING FOR A MORTGAGE

It's amazing how far you've come. By now, you know how much you can afford to spend on a home. You know how much cash you have on hand for a down payment, closing costs, and a cushion. And you've found yourself a mortgage advisor who can help you through the process of actually getting a mortgage. So let's get going. You're ready to decide which mortgage is the right fit for you.

AUTOMATIC MILLIONAIRE HOMEOWNER ACTION STEPS

Reviewing the actions we laid out in this chapter, here's what you should be doing right now to find yourself a mortgage advisor you can trust—and get yourself ready to start shopping for a home.

❏ See if you know anyone who can recommend a mortgage banker or broker they've worked with.

❏ Check the newspaper ads for a mortgage advisor who seems right for you and make an appointment to see him or her. Do the same at your bank.

❏ Based on your research and your meetings with at least one mortgage banker and one mortgage broker, select a mortgage advisor to work with.

❏ Go to **www.finishrich.com/ homeowner/chapterfour** to listen to the free audio supplement to this chapter.

CHAPTER FIVE

THE AUTOMATIC MILLIONAIRE HOMEOWNER RIGHT-FIT MORTGAGE PLAN

There are literally thousands of different kinds of mortgages to choose from. The question is, which one is the right fit for you? Don't worry if you have no idea how to answer that question. By the time you finish reading this chapter, you will.

So exactly what is a mortgage? Very simply, it's a loan you get—usually from a bank or other financial institution, but sometimes from the seller—so you can buy a house or other piece of real estate. What makes it a mortgage as opposed to an ordinary loan is that the collateral you put up to guarantee repayment happens to be the real estate you're using it to buy.

Let's say you decide to buy a home for $200,000, and let's say you've got enough money in the bank so you can pay 20 percent of the purchase price in cash ($40,000). That means you will need to borrow $160,000 to close the deal. This $160,000 loan will be your mortgage. You pay the seller $40,000 in cash, the lender gives him another $160,000, and you get legal title to the house—with one catch. If you fail to pay off the mortgage as promised, the lender can foreclose, evict you from the premises, and recoup what cash it can by having the sheriff auction off what used to be—but no longer is—your property.

Assuming you do make your payments on time, you will eventually build up what's called equity in your home. Your equity is basically the amount of your home's value that belongs to you. You calculate it by taking the home's fair market value and subtracting how much you owe on any mortgages you've taken out against it. Going back to the example I used above, if you've got a $160,000 mortgage on a house that's worth $200,000, you will have $40,000 in equity (which makes sense, since that's exactly the amount of the cash down payment you made). There are actually two ways to build equity—one is by paying off your mortgage, and the other is when your home goes up in value.

THE 1-2-3'S OF HOME FINANCING—HOW A MORTGAGE WORKS

Mortgages have three basic components. There's the size of the mortgage (how much you're borrowing), the term of the mortgage (how much time you have to pay it off), and the cost of the mortgage (how much interest the lender is charging you). Most mortgages have terms of either 15 or

30 years (the choice is yours), while the interest rate depends on the current state of the national economy as well as your financial condition, credit record, and whether or not you plan to occupy the home you are buying.

When you are applying for a mortgage, your broker or banker may prepare a payment timetable—known as an amortization schedule—that shows how your monthly payments will be applied against your debt. Except in the case of what are called "interest only" mortgages (which I'll explain later), part of each payment will cover the interest charges you owe, while the rest will go to pay back what you actually borrowed—what bankers call the **principal.** Generally speaking, in the early years of a mortgage, the interest part of your monthly payment is much bigger than the principal part. But as time goes on and the amount of principal you still owe begins to decline, the proportion shifts, and more of each payment goes to paying off the principal balance—until, at the very end, virtually everything is going to the principal and hardly anything to interest.

This is important to know because when it comes to your home (as opposed to a rental property), the interest portion of your mortgage payment is usually tax-deductible; the principal part isn't. Another reason to pay attention to the amortization schedule is that, as we will see in Chapter Nine, you can save big money by paying down your mortgage faster than the schedule calls for. (However, some mortgages have restrictions on the size of your payment and include what are called "prepayment penalties," which charge you extra if you want to pay off your mortgage early. As a rule, you should try to avoid mortgages that carry these kinds of penalties, unless they come with a benefit you need.)

WHAT KINDS OF MORTGAGES ARE AVAILABLE—AND WHICH ONE IS BEST FOR YOU?

This is where the journey starts to get exhilarating—and maybe a little scary.

Shopping for a mortgage can be exhilarating because in recent years the mortgage lending industry has come up with all sorts of creative products that make it easier for people not only to buy a home but also to buy more of a home because they can borrow more money.

It's sometimes scary for pretty much the same reason. There are so many new mortgage products and styles of financing that it can make your head spin. And if you're not careful and pick the wrong type of mortgage, you can get hurt.

The good news here is that while there are more choices than ever, there are only a few factors that determine which is the right fit for you. Do you like taking risks or are you conservative? How long do you expect to own the house you're planning to buy? Is your income stream steady or erratic? Do you expect your income to grow significantly, or is your career mature? Do you have the cash for a down payment?

We'll start by looking at the most basic kinds of mortgages, then move to the more creative and exciting products—all with an eye toward which may be best for you.

Ready?

Great—let's go.

FIXED-RATE MORTGAGES

Fixed-rate mortgages are the industry's most basic mortgage product. Most have a term of either 15 years or 30 years—30 being by far the most popular. (That's because, in order to pay off the loan in half the time, the monthly payments on a 15-year mortgage are roughly 35 percent to 40 percent higher than those on a 30-year mortgage.)

The defining characteristic of the fixed-rate mortgage is that its interest rate is fixed for the term of the loan. So however long you sign up for (15 years, 30 years, or whatever), the bank is guaranteeing that your interest rate—and, along with it, the size of your monthly payment—won't change. When mortgage interest rates are low, locking in a rate for 15 or 30 years can be really smart—particularly if you think you're going to be living in the home for more than five years. It's certainly the conservative way to go. With a fixed rate, you never lose sleep worrying that your monthly payment might go up. It can't—because it's fixed!

Fixed-rate mortgages are also attractive when you don't expect your income to go up very much in the future—say, because you've pretty much gone as far as you're going to go in your career, or because either you or your spouse are planning to stop working.

On page 159 is an important chart that shows where mortgage rates have been over the last half-century. You can see they were lower in the 2000–2005 period than at any time in the previous forty years.

As I write this in the summer of 2005, with rates on 30-year mortgages running

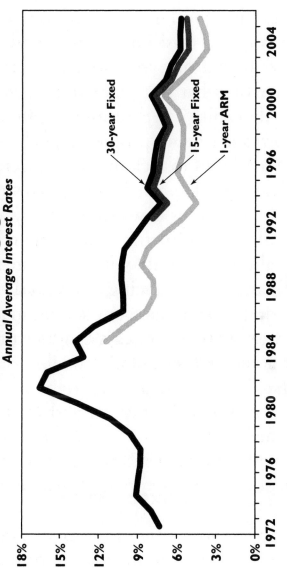

Historical Mortgage Rates
Annual Average Interest Rates

30-year Fixed
15-year Fixed
1-year ARM

Rates shown are commitment rates for conventional, conforming loans.
The adjustable-rate mortgage survey began in 1984; the 15-year fixed-rate survey began in 1991.
Averages for 2005 are through October 20.
Source: Freddie Mac

around 5.75 percent, I happen to think now is a GREAT time to lock in a long-term fixed rate. But who knows where rates will be when you read this? Look at the chart on page 159. It will give you some historical perspective on what to think about current rates. If they hit 7.5 percent for 30-year fixed mortgages, many people may tell you they are "too high" to lock in now. In fact, if you look at the table, you'll see that, historically, 7.5 percent is low. And if they do drop significantly sometime down the road (as they almost certainly will), you can always refinance. (Refinancing can sometimes cost you quite a bit in fees, but if you can get a much better interest rate, it can be worth it over the term of the loan.)

Is a fixed-rate mortgage the right fit for you? Let's consider the 30-year and 15-year versions separately.

30-YEAR FIXED RATE

Pro: Locks in your interest rate, so you're protected if rates rise. Payments are the same each month. Easy to track and monitor and make automatic.

Con: You are locked into a rate for 30 years, which means if rates fall, you'll miss out on savings unless you refinance.

Bottom Line: If you are conservative, value peace of mind, and are planning on being in your home a long time (at least seven to ten years), a 30-year fixed rate mortgage offers the most benefits.

15-YEAR FIXED RATE

Pro: The interest rate on a 15-year mortgage is lower than that on a 30-year. You pay off your home and become debt-free in 15 years. Also easy to track, monitor, and automate.

Con: Monthly payments are higher than with a 30-year mortgage.

Bottom Line: If you are a really committed saver and plan to live in your home longer than ten years, this is the loan for you. You can lock in a rate and be debt-free in a decade and a half.

ADJUSTABLE-RATE MORTGAGES (ARMs)

Adjustable-rate mortgages, usually referred to as ARMs, are typically 30-year mortgages whose interest rate is fixed for a set period of time that is less than the full term. The most popular variety is what is known as a 5/1 ARM. This means that the rate you get at the start is fixed only for the first five years. After that, it is adjusted once a year (this is what the "1" means), based on the movement of a key economic indicator (such as the Treasury Bill, LIBOR, or Cost of Funds Index) that is specified in the mortgage agreement. Also popular are 7/1 and 10/1 ARMs, in which the interest rate is fixed for an initial period of seven and 10 years, respectively. There are also short-term ARMs, with rates that are locked for periods as short as one month, six months, one year, or three years.

WHY PEOPLE LIKE ARMS

The advantage of ARMs is that they generally offer lower interest rates than comparable fixed-rate mortgages—at least for that initial period. The disadvantage is that once the initial period ends, all bets are off. If interest rates rise, your monthly payment will go up along with them. And if they keep rising, so will your payment. On the other hand, if rates fall, your payment will go down. ARMs have worked out extremely well for homeowners in the 2000–2005 period because during this time rates went down and stayed down. But things can change. Between 2004 and mid-2005, the Federal Reserve raised the federal funds rate twelve times, and now the rates on most ARMs are starting to go up, as well. The thing to remember is that there are no guarantees. So if you don't like uncertainty, or if you can't count on having more money to spend on your mortgage than you have right now, ARMs are not for you.

MAKE SURE TO ASK ABOUT THE
MARGIN ON YOUR LOAN

The way adjustable-rate mortgages adjust can seem complicated, but the process is actually quite straightforward if you know what to look for. If you have an ARM, most likely your mortgage agreement will say something like this: Your rate will be 5 percent for five years, after which it will adjust to 2.5 percent over the treasury index or

WARNING—
THE DANGER OF ARMS

Amid the explosion of mortgage opportunities, my biggest concern is that too many people are taking out short-term ARMs with very low initial rates so they can buy homes that are more expensive than they can really afford. If rates go up, many of these buyers may be priced out of their homes by their rapidly rising mortgage payments. On page 165 is a table that shows what can happen if you have an ARM in a rising-rate environment.

whatever index your particular loan happens to use. This 2.5 percent is what is known as the margin.

MONTHLY PRINCIPAL & INTEREST PAYMENTS ON A 1-YEAR ADJUSTABLE-RATE MORTGAGE AS RATES RISE						
Assuming a 5% Initial Rate and a 0.5% Annual Increase						
		Original Loan Amount				
Year	Rate	$100,000	$200,000	$300,000	$400,000	$500,000
1	5.0%	$537	$1,074	$1,610	$2,147	$2,684
2	5.5%	$567	$1,134	$1,701	$2,268	$2,835
3	6.0%	$597	$1,195	$1,792	$2,389	$2,987
4	6.5%	$628	$1,255	$1,883	$2,510	$3,138
5	7.0%	$658	$1,315	$1,973	$2,631	$3,288
6	7.5%	$688	$1,375	$2,063	$2,750	$3,438
7	8.0%	$717	$1,435	$2,152	$2,870	$3,587
8	8.5%	$747	$1,494	$2,241	$2,988	$3,734
9	9.0%	$776	$1,552	$2,328	$3,104	$3,880
10	9.5%	$805	$1,610	$2,415	$3,220	$4,025

Say your index rate is 5 percent when your initial five years is up. Adding the 2.5 percent margin to that would bring your mortgage interest rate to 7.5 percent—an increase of 50 percent! After years of low interest rates, this may seem hard to believe—but trust me, just as rates fall, so, too, do they rise.

When shopping for adjustable-rate mortgages, there are three things to consider: comparing the margins, the initial rates, and the length of the fixed term before making any decisions.

Is an adjustable-rate mortgage the right fit for you? Let's consider short-term and intermediate-term ARMs separately.

SHORT-TERM ARMS
(THREE YEARS OR LESS)

Pro: You get a substantial break on the interest rate at first, so initially at least the monthly payment will be much less with this mortgage than with most other loans.

Con: If interest rates go up quickly, you can find yourself having trouble making the payments.

Bottom Line: A great deal if rates stay low, short-term ARMs make sense for homebuyers who want to keep their monthly payments as small as possible, can handle risk, and don't expect to live in the house more than a few years. But not a good idea if you expect interest rates to rise in the near future and you don't expect your income to rise along with them.

INTERMEDIATE ARMS
(5/1, 7/1, OR 10/1)

Pro: Relatively low rates.

Con: Your rate is locked only for a limited time. After that, if rates have risen, your monthly mortgage payment will rise.

Bottom Line: Intermediate ARMs are great for a homebuyer who is looking for lower monthly payments and is either not planning on keeping the property very long or expects rates to rise for a while but eventually fall.

"NO DOWN PAYMENT" AND "PIGGYBACK" MORTGAGES

Remember in the Introduction, when I shared the story of Karen and how she wanted to buy a piece of real estate after reading a book on it? We got into a discussion about whether or not you really can buy a home with "no money down" the way the infomercials say you can. I wound up polling the room and found that out of a hundred people, only two people had actually done it.

Well, that was nearly ten years ago. If I took a poll like that now, the results would be very different. That's because these days numerous national banks and other respectable lending institutions offer incredibly simple "no money down" home mortgages—and thousands of homebuyers have been signing up for them. Indeed, according to the National Association of Realtors, between the beginning of 2004 and the middle of 2005, roughly one out of every three new homeowners bought his or her house with a "no money down" mortgage.

So if you are interested in buying a home sooner rather than later and you don't have a lot of money saved for a down payment, you should visit the local branch of a national bank or mortgage company and ask them if they have any "no money down" loan programs for first-time homebuyers. You may be pleasantly surprised to find that they do and you qualify.

UNDERSTAND THE RISKS OF "NO DOWN PAYMENT" MORTGAGES

What can go wrong with borrowing the entire purchase price of a home? The answer is simple: If real estate values drop and you have no equity in your house, you can find yourself **owing more than your place is worth!** Should you be forced to sell your home under these circumstances, you wouldn't be able to get enough from the sale to cover what you owe the bank.

This is commonly referred to as being

"upside down" in your real estate holdings. You'd be surprised how easily this can happen when things go wrong. So far in this book, I've given you examples of how the leverage you get from borrowing money to buy a home can make you rich in a rising market. Let me show how it can quickly make you poor in a falling one.

Say you buy a home for $300,000. The bank loans you the entire purchase price (all $300,000), so you don't have to put anything down. Everything is going great. You're comfortable making your mortgage payments. Your family loves the home. You're planning to live there for at least ten years. Life is wonderful.

Then one day you go to work and find out that your company has been acquired by a competitor. A week later you are let go.

No longer able to make your mortgage payments, you put your home up for sale. Unfortunately, the market has cooled. You try to sell the house for $300,000, which is what you paid for it (and owe the bank), but there are no takers. After three months, you lower the price to $275,000. It finally sells for $260,000. After paying the 6 percent commission to the real estate agents, you collect $244,400. That's $56,000 short of what you need to be able to pay back the bank. You don't have $56,000, so now what? This is when some people find themselves facing bankruptcy.

This scenario may seem unbelievably bad, but all it assumes is that real estate prices dropped by 15 percent. In the first six months of 2005, real estate prices nationally went up by 15 percent! Think they can't go down 15 percent in six months? Think again.

I'm not telling you this to scare you off from buying a home with no money down. For many readers of this book, the ability to get a "no down payment" mortgage may be the difference between being able to buy a home now and having to continue to throw money away on rent for years to come. I happen to believe that it's worth stretching yourself in order to get out of the rent rut. But you need to know the risks. And there are risks!

So if you plan to buy with no money

down, consider your backup plan. If you suddenly lost your job and your income, would you be able to pay your mortgage until you got back on your feet again? Or might you be forced into a quick—and potentially disastrous—sale? Unless you have a secure safety net—like the possibility of a loan from your family or assets you could liquidate in an emergency or a payment plan you can work out with your mortgage company—a "no money down" mortgage may be too risky for you.

THE PIGGYBACK OPTION

There is a middle ground between the risk of a "no down payment" mortgage and the expense of a standard mortgage with its 20 percent down payment requirement. What are generally known as "low down payment" products are becoming increasingly common, the most popular of them being what are called 80/10/10 and 80/15/5 loans—or more familiarly, piggyback mortgages.

The 80/10/10 loan allows you to buy a

house with a down payment of only 10 percent of the purchase price: You get a regular mortgage that covers 80 percent of the purchase price, and piggybacked on top of that is a second mortgage or home equity loan— also known as a "line" (as in line of credit)— that covers the remaining 10 percent. It's the same deal with an 80/15/5 loan, except that the home equity line covers 15 percent of the purchase price, reducing your down payment to only 5 percent.

While second mortgages can be adjustable or fixed, home equity lines almost always have adjustable rates. They generally float up and down with the Prime Rate, so even if your underlying mortgage is a fixed-rate loan, your total monthly payment may be subject to change. Make sure to ask your advisor whether or not yours is. Then again, since the home equity portion represents a relatively small percentage of your total obligation, the variation from month to month is not likely to be large.

THERE'S A CATCH WITH LOW AND NO DOWN PAYMENT MORTGAGES: PRIVATE MORTGAGE INSURANCE

Because it's riskier to loan money to people who make small down payments, lenders require homebuyers who borrow more than 80 percent of the cost of their house to purchase what is called private mortgage insurance, or PMI. PMI covers any losses the lender may incur in the event a borrower defaults, and it is not cheap. Depending on the size of your mortgage and how small a down payment you made, it can run anywhere from $50 to several hundred dollars a month. (The cost is generally added to your monthly mortgage payment.)

Fortunately, there are a number of ways to avoid having to buy PMI—even if you have a low down payment mortgage.

THREE WAYS TO AVOID THE PMI REQUIREMENT

1. **Buy your house with a "piggyback" mortgage** like the 80/10/10 or 80/15/5 loans I described earlier. Some lenders will consider the 10 percent or 15 percent home equity portion of the loan as the equivalent of a cash down payment, thus allowing you to avoid the PMI requirement.

2. **Pay down your mortgage** sufficiently to get the loan-to-value ratio below 80 percent (meaning the size of your mortgage is less than 80 percent of your home's appraised value). Normally, this might take years, but making extra payments can accelerate the process. And though this might be painful, it could be worth your while.

3. **Keep a close eye on your home's market value.** As it rises above what you paid for it, your loan-to-value ratio will drop. For example, if you were to buy a house worth $100,000 by putting

down $10,000 in cash and getting a $90,000 mortgage, your initial loan-to-value ratio would be 90 percent, and you would have to buy PMI. But say the value of your house were to rise to $120,000. Now your $90,000 mortgage would represent only 75 percent of the house's value, and you would no longer need PMI. So keep tabs on what your house is worth and, as soon as you think its value is high enough, have the place reappraised. If you've calculated correctly, you should be able to get this insurance requirement waived. (Of course, if prices later fall and you haven't paid off sufficient principal, your lender could insist on re-imposing the PMI requirement.)

Is a "no down payment" or "piggyback" mortgage the right fit for you?

Pro: You can buy a home without having to save up—or plunk down—a bundle.

Con: You start out with very little, if any, equity; and if prices fall, you could find yourself owing more than your house is worth. You also may be required to purchase private mortgage insurance.

Bottom Line: A great alternative if you're drowning in rent and lack substantial savings—but only if your income is steady and your job is secure.

INTEREST-ONLY MORTGAGES

In an effort to attract business by keeping monthly payments as low as possible, more and more lenders are offering mortgages that permit you to pay only the interest charges on your loan—and not, as is usually the case, the interest plus some of the principal. Interest-only payment plans covering the first five, 10, or even 15 years of the loan are available for just about every type of mortgage, including all the varieties I've described so far. In 2004, more than 30 percent of all mortgages were interest-only.

The main reason this feature is so popular is that it allows people to buy a more expensive house than they could otherwise afford, since it drops the monthly payment below that of a standard mortgage. For example, let's say you'd need a $300,000 loan to buy the house you want. With a standard 30-year fixed mortgage at 6 percent, you'd be looking at a monthly payment of just under $1,800. But with an interest-only plan, the cost during the initial interest-only phase would be just $1,500 a month.

Reducing your mortgage costs in this way certainly seems attractive, and it can make sense if you're not planning to own the house for very long and are confident its value is going to increase. It's also appropriate if you believe you can get a better return by putting the money you're saving into the stock market or some other kind of investment. However—and this is a very big "however"—there are some huge drawbacks to interest-only mortgages.

For one thing, if you keep the house (and your interest-only mortgage) longer than the interest-only period, you could find yourself facing some uncomfortably high monthly payments. That's because once you do begin paying down the principal on an interest-only mortgage, you have to pay it off at a faster rate than normal in order to be able to retire the loan on time.

For another, interest-only mortgages **are interest-only**. Paying only the interest may sound great, but it also means that you're **not** paying off any principal, which means that you're not building any equity.

Say you buy a home for $300,000 and you borrow the entire purchase price with a no down payment, interest-only 6 percent mortgage. (Yes, there are mortgages like this.) Over ten years, you will pay the lender $180,000 in interest—but at the end of that time, you will still owe him $300,000. Now, if the value of the house has risen over the years to $600,000, this may not bother you. But if its value hasn't gone up—or, worse, if it has gone down—you are going to be really disappointed.

Is an interest-only mortgage the right fit for you?

Pro: During the initial interest-only period, your monthly payments will be significantly lower than they would be for a similarly sized standard mortgage. In a rising market, a great way to maximize your leverage.

Con: You don't build equity unless your house appreciates in value—and you could face "sticker shock" when the interest-only period ends.

Bottom Line: Interest-only mortgages make sense if you're planning to own the home for a relatively short period of time (say, less than five years) and have a good use for the money you'll save. But using one simply to buy a bigger house than you can really afford is a recipe for disaster.

OPTION MORTGAGES

Option mortgages are short-term ARMs that allow you to decide each month what kind of mortgage payment you would like to make during the initial period of the loan. Depending on how you're feeling—or, more likely, the state of your bank account—you can make a payment as if you had a traditional ARM with a 30-year term, you can make an interest-only payment, or you can choose what's called the "deferred interest option," in which you make a monthly payment that covers none of the principal and not even all the interest you owe. (The unpaid or "deferred" interest is simply put on your tab—that is, it's added to the total amount you owe.)

The array of choices you get with an option mortgage can be very helpful if your income is erratic, since it allows you to cut your monthly mortgage payments way back in some months and then increase them in others. The danger is that it's tempting to keep choosing that deferred interest option with its very low monthly payment (sometimes as low as half the standard payment). This is called "negative amortization." Do this consistently and you'll wind up **owing more than you actually borrowed**. If your house goes up in value, you won't mind this. In fact, you might even feel brilliant, since you'd have managed to accumulate a lot of equity while paying out very little cash. On the other hand, if the value of your house doesn't appreciate—or, worse, actually declines—you could easily end up "upside down" in terms of your home equity, owing more on your house than it is worth, despite years of payments. That's a pretty brutal prospect.

Of all the different types of mortgages, the option mortgage is probably the most complicated. Yet because it seems so flexible, it's becoming more and more popular. A lot of people are using these mortgages to finance the purchase of investment properties because the low monthly payments make it easier to generate a positive cash flow.

My feeling is that option mortgages can be a very attractive proposition for a disciplined homebuyer, but—and this is a very big "but"—you need to understand what you are getting yourself into. Carefully review the risks associated with this loan with your mortgage advisor. Have your advisor show you what can happen if you make the minimum payments on this loan for, say, three years and then rates go up by 1 percent or 2 percent. Then think long and hard about whether you are really comfortable with the risk.

A NOTE ON RISK

Many of today's innovative mortgage products emerged in a time of skyrocketing home prices—an environment in which people could reasonably expect to "flip" properties so quickly that they would never have to worry about feeling the bite of a rising adjustable rate or finding themselves "upside down" in a falling market. This kind of party may be fun while it lasts, but it never lasts forever. Indeed, as I write this, the current one seems to be winding down. An Automatic Millionaire Homeowner is a long-term buyer who plans to live in his house for many years like the Martins did and weather the cycles of a real estate market that goes up AND down. **This means getting yourself a mortgage that makes sense for the long term.**

Is an option mortgage the right fit for you?

Pro: Great flexibility, including the ability to cut your monthly payments in half in the short term.

Con: If you're not careful, you could easily find yourself both "upside down" or facing unmanageable payments when the option period ends.

Bottom Line: Option mortgages can be great if you're a disciplined investor with an erratic income stream. But if you don't understand the risks, you could easily end up in a world of surprise and hurt.

THE GOVERNMENT WANTS YOU TO BE A HOMEOWNER

So far, we've been concentrating on what's available from banks and mortgage companies. Now let's look at what the government can do to help you buy a home. You may be

THE EFFECTS OF DIFFERENT "OPTION" MORTGAGE PAYMENTS

Assuming a 5% Initial Rate and Annual Adjustment

Year	Rate	Monthly Payment: Traditional ARM payment	Monthly Payment: Interest only payment	Monthly Payment: Deferred option (minimum payment)	Remaining Balance, End of Year: Traditional ARM payment	Remaining Balance, End of Year: Interest only payment	Remaining Balance, End of Year: Deferred option (minimum payment)
1	5.00%	$1,074	$833	$675	$197,049	$200,000	$201,944
2	6.00%	$1,196	$1,000	$700	$194,448	$200,000	$203,681
3	7.00%	$1,321	$1,167	$725	$192,128	$200,000	$205,199
4	8.00%	$1,449	$1,333	$750	$190,033	$200,000	$206,489
5	8.00%	$1,449	$1,333	$775	$187,763	$200,000	$207,537
6	8.00%	$1,449	$1,544	$1,602	$185,763	$197,382	$204,820
7	8.00%	$1,449	$1,544	$1,602	$182,643	$191,999	$199,235

Note: Each column has been calculated assuming that the borrower will make payments of the same type consistently for an initial five-year option period. In year six, when the option period has ended, payments are determined by the outstanding principal balance, and assume an 8% interest rate over the 25 years remaining on the loan term.   Source: Wells Fargo Home Mortgage surprised by just how much Uncle Sam wants you to become a homeowner. That's because homeownership is not only good for individuals, it's also good for the national economy. It creates wealth, lends stability to communities, increases the tax base, and stimulates business activity.

And don't think government housing programs are just for poor people. Many of these programs are aimed at working people with household incomes anywhere from 80 percent to 120 percent of their area's median—which, in big, expensive cities like Boston, Chicago, Los Angeles, and New York, can easily include families that earn well over $50,000 a year. So check them out.

HOW HUD MAKES HOMEBUYING EASIER

Housing and Urban Development (HUD)
www.hud.gov

The mission of the U.S. Department of Housing and Urban Development (HUD) is to create opportunities for homeownership. To this end, it offers all kinds of assistance to would-be homebuyers, including grants to help people buy a first home.

The HUD web site, at **www.hud.gov**, is where you should really start your research on government programs. It offers a wealth of resources on how to buy, what kind of help you can get, and how to qualify for assistance, as well as links to hundreds of state and local programs aimed at making home-ownership easier. Especially useful are the **100 Questions & Answers About Buying a New Home.** You can even chat online with an agency representative and be referred to a housing counselor in your area.

OTHER GOVERNMENT AGENCIES THAT CAN HELP YOU BECOME A HOMEOWNER

In addition to HUD, there are a number of other government agencies that offer lending programs and other assistance that every potential homebuyer should investigate.

Federal Housing Administration
www.fha.com

Since 1934, the FHA has helped more than 30 million people become homeowners—not by lending them money but by guaranteeing their loans, thus reassuring lenders who may be reluctant to make loans to buyers who don't have a lot of money. FHA-guaranteed loans often cover up to 97 percent of the purchase price, and though they are usually meant for first homes, they can also be used to buy second or third homes. As of this writing, the FHA was willing to guarantee mortgage loans up to $359,650. (The ceiling is always being increased, so be sure to check.)

U.S. Department of Veterans Affairs
www.va.gov

If you served in the armed forces, you can get a mortgage guaranteed by the VA—which usually means a lower interest rate than you'd otherwise get. Details are available at the VA's web site.

National Council of State Housing Finance Agencies

www.ncsha.org

Virtually every state in the union offers special loan programs to help homebuyers, particularly first-timers. The NCSHA web site is a great way to find out all about them.

Fannie Mae

www.fanniemae.com

1-800-832-2345

The Federal National Mortgage Association, otherwise known as Fannie Mae, doesn't lend money itself. What it does is provide the financing that makes it possible for banks to lend money to consumers. It also offers lots of good information for consumers, including an entire library of FREE reports with titles like **Choosing a Mortgage, Knowing Your Credit, and Borrowing Basics.** In addition, check out **www. homepath.com**, a related Fannie Mae web site that contains a consumer-friendly "For Home Buyers & Homeowners" section filled with helpful information.

Freddie Mac

www.freddiemac.com

1-800-373-3343

Fannie Mae's younger cousin, Freddie Mac (a.k.a. the Federal Home Loan Mortgage Corporation), provides the financing that allows lenders to offer home loans that are affordable. The Freddie Mac web site has a terrific section for would-be homebuyers (at **www.freddiemac.com/homebuyers**), where you'll find a wonderful tool called "The Road to Home Ownership." It also has a related web site at **www.homesteps.com** that helps first-time homebuyers find bargain homes, get one-step loan approvals, and learn how to buy foreclosed properties with as little as 5 percent down.

CONGRATULATIONS— YOU ARE NOW OVER THE HARD PART

As I said at the beginning of this chapter, there are enough mortgage products out there to make your head spin. But now you know how to find the one that is the right fit for you. The hardest part is behind you. In the next chapter, we're going to look at how to get you the best mortgage deal possible.

Keep going—you are doing great!

AUTOMATIC MILLIONAIRE HOMEOWNER ACTION STEPS

Reviewing the actions we laid out in this chapter, here's what you should be doing right now to determine which type of mortgage is the right fit for you.

❑ Understand that before you start shopping for a house, you need to shop for a mortgage.

❑ Based on the criteria laid out in this chapter, decide which type of mortgage product makes sense for you.

❑ Visit the various government web sites listed on pages 186 to 191 to see if you qualify for any government programs aimed at would-be homebuyers.

❑ Go to **www.finishrich.com/ homeowner/chapterfive** to listen to the free audio supplement to this chapter.

CHAPTER SIX

HOW TO GET THE BEST DEAL ON YOUR MORTGAGE

Now that you know the kinds of mortgages out there, it's time for you to go shopping for a mortgage for you. And when I say go shopping, I mean it.

When you go out to make a major purchase—say, a new car or a big appliance—you don't simply walk into the first showroom you see and accept the first price the salesman quotes you. A good shopper goes to a number of different stores, compares offers, and even plays competing retailers against each other.

The same applies when you're shopping for a mortgage. Before you start considering offers, you need to have a good sense of what kinds of deals are available. And don't think that you can skip this part just because you've found yourself a mortgage advisor you can trust. Remember Ronald Reagan's advice about doing business when the stakes are high: "Trust, but verify."

What this means is that you need to do a little research.

DO SOME COMPARISON SHOPPING IN THE NEWSPAPERS AND ONLINE

These days it's easier than ever to find out what's happening in the mortgage markets. Just pick up your local newspaper. Most have a weekly real estate section that routinely includes a table of average rates for different kinds of mortgages. The real estate section also tends to be chock full of advertisements from various lending institutions touting their best offers for certain products. So make a note of what's being advertised and where rates currently are.

After that, I would go online to do some investigative shopping. In a matter of minutes, you can become aware of different loan products and their pricing—and when it comes to getting a good deal, knowledge is power. My favorite mortgage-shopping web sites are:

WEB SITES TO SHOP FOR A MORTGAGE

www.ameriquestmortgage. com

www.bankrate.com

www.countrywide.com

www.ditech.com

www.eloan.com

www.interest.com

www.lendingtree.com

www.quickenloans.com

www.bankofamerica.com

www.chase.com

www.citibank.com

www.suntrust.com

www.usbank.com

www.wachovia.com

www.wamu.com

www.wellsfargo.com

Spend an hour browsing these web sites—both the ones that compare mortgages like **www.bankrate.com** and **www. eloan.com** and the ones run by national banks like **www.wellsfargo.com** or **www. citibank.com**—and you will quickly get a sense of what kinds of deals are out there. In turn, this should give you some perspective on the deals your mortgage advisor may recommend to you. If the deals your advisor brings you don't seem as attractive as what you've seen in the newspapers or online, don't hesitate to ask why. In many cases, you may find that's because the rates quoted in the ads are for products that won't suit your needs. Or maybe you missed the fine print, and what you thought were really great deals in the newspapers or online aren't really so great after all. But don't assume that. Ask.

THE HOLY GRAIL OF MORTGAGE LENDING

You might be surprised to know that before you ever meet with a mortgage advisor you've already begun the process of determining what kind of mortgage you are going to be able to get. In fact, you started that process long before you ever even thought about trying to buy a home.

From the time you got your first credit card or took out your first student loan, you've been compiling what's known as a credit history. And it's your credit history, along with your income, assets, and liabilities, that will govern whether you can get a great deal on a mortgage or one that's not so great.

In the next few pages, we'll look at how lenders weigh your credit history—and then how you can make the most of it to get yourself the best possible deal on a mortgage.

UNDERSTANDING YOUR "FINANCIAL GPA"

It's funny how little time our schools spend teaching us about the simple things that really matter in the world. When you were in high school, did anyone ever bring up the subject of credit scores? More than likely not. The only score that mattered was your GPA—your grade point average. Well, what about your financial GPA—your credit score? The fact is that when it comes time to borrow money for anything—whether it's a house, a car, or your children's education— the first thing any lender will do is pull your credit score.

Your credit score is a number that the major credit-rating agencies calculate for you based on your credit history. Banks use this number to determine whether they will lend you money and, if so, what kind of interest rate they will charge. For mortgage lenders—and borrowers—it's the Holy Grail. A high number means you've got a good credit history and, hence, are a good risk, so you'll likely qualify for loans at relatively low interest rates. A low number means you're a bad risk and will, as a result, probably have to pay a much higher interest rate—that is, if the bank is willing to lend you any money at all.

HOW YOUR CREDIT SCORE WORKS—AND WHY IT MATTERS

The most influential credit-scoring system was developed back in 1989 by a company called Fair Isaac Corp. The idea was to give lenders a quick and easy way to judge an individual's creditworthiness. What they call your FICO score is a mathematical calculation based on 22 pieces of data about you that Fair Isaac gets from Equifax, Experian, and TransUnion, the three main credit-reporting companies. Based on this calculation, you are rated on a scale that ranges from 350 (the lowest) to 850 (the highest). Anything over 700 is considered good. Score 750 or higher and the lenders will give you their best deals. On the other hand, a score below 500 means you will have trouble getting a loan no matter how high an interest rate you're willing to pay. The table on page 200 is similar to one you'll find on the FICO web site that shows how differing credit scores can affect your interest rate.

HOW CREDIT SCORES AFFECT YOUR INTEREST RATE		
(based on a $150,000 30-year, fixed-rate mortgage, as of 7/31/05)		
Score	Interest Rate	Monthly Payment
760–850	5.48%	$850
700–759	5.7%	$871
680–699	5.88%	$887
660–679	6.09%	$908
640–459	6.52%	$950
620–639	7.07%	$1,005

As you can see, the difference between a low score and a high score can make a difference of hundreds of dollars in mortgage interest payments each month—and tens, if not hundreds, of thousands of dollars over the life of the loan.

HOW TO FIND OUT YOUR CREDIT SCORE—AND MORE

Knowing how you rate is essential knowledge for anyone even thinking of getting a mortgage. There are a number of ways to find out your credit score. To begin with, you can get it directly from Fair Isaac. You can also get a version of your FICO score from the three credit bureaus, which all have credit scoring systems similar to Fair Isaac's. Let's take a look at what each has to offer.

Fair Isaac Corp.

www.myfico.com

Visitors to the Fair Isaac web site can purchase (for $44.85) what the firm calls its FICO Deluxe service, which includes copies of your credit reports from all three credit bureaus as well as your FICO score. You actually have three separate credit scores and credit histories (compiled by each of the bureaus listed on the next page). The FICO Deluxe report shows you what they all say about you and what you can do to improve your score.

Equifax

www.equifax.com

(800) 685-1111

Equifax offers several products and combinations of products ranging from $9.50 for a copy of your Equifax credit report to $39.95 for its 3-in-1 report with Score-Power® (your FICO credit score and your credit report from all three agencies plus a comparison of how your score stacks up to national averages and a simulator that shows how changes to your credit report could impact your credit score).

Experian

www.experian.com
(888) 397-3742

Like Equifax, Experian offers several combinations of products and services, ranging from your Experian credit report for $9.50 to a "3 Bureau" credit report that includes your credit score for $34.95.

TransUnion Corporation

www.transunion.com
(800) 888-4213

Like the others, TransUnion offers a basic credit report for $9.50 and a 3-in-1 credit profile for $29.95.

YOU CAN NOW GET YOUR CREDIT REPORT FOR FREE

Under the Fair and Accurate Credit Transaction Act of 2003, the three big credit bureaus must provide every consumer who asks with a free copy of their credit report once a year. You can get yours by contacting them directly or by going to a web site they jointly sponsor at **www.annualcredit report.com**. You can also mail in a request to Annual Credit Report Request Service at P.O. Box 105283, Atlanta, GA 30348-5283, or call them toll-free at (877) 322-8228.

As I indicated earlier, each credit bureau has its own records and issues its own report, so you need to go to each of them for a copy of what they're saying about you. And keep in mind that your credit report is not your credit score! They are different. Your score is **based** on your reports—and, unfortunately, you can't get it for free.

CHANCES ARE, THERE'S A MISTAKE IN YOUR REPORT

Having coached thousands of people on the process of both pulling and fixing their credit scores, I can tell you from experience that you will probably find some incorrect information in your credit report. **Since these mistakes often make your credit history look worse than it really is, it's vitally important that you get them corrected as soon as possible.**

It's actually not very difficult to do this. You can report any errors you find directly to the credit bureau whose report contained the mistake by going online to its web site. At the same time, however, you should document your complaint by sending the credit bureau a letter via certified mail.

By law, the credit bureaus have to investigate and correct your score within 30 days of receiving your notice. I've posted some sample letters you can use at **www.automatic millionairecredit.com**.

> ## A SPECIAL DISCOUNT—
> ## AND A GIFT—FOR YOU
>
> Because understanding your credit history is so
> important, I'm working with the bureaus to get
> you discounts on the fees the bureaus normally
> charge consumers who want to find out their
> credit scores. If you go online and visit **www.
> automaticmillionairecredit.com**, you'll be
> sent to a web site where you'll be able to take
> advantage of special offers—and also download
> some additional free resources, including a
> special report I created in audio format called
> **How to Fix Your Credit Score—and
> Improve It in 60 Days or Less.**

DON'T BE AFRAID TO ASK FOR A
BETTER DEAL ON YOUR
CLOSING COSTS

Improving your credit score might take
some time, but there's another way to make
sure you get a great deal. Ask. The simplest
way to cut the cost of your mortgage is to
ask for a better deal. You may not be able

to get a better interest rate, but particularly when the loan is large, my experience is that a lender will often agree to give you a break on at least some of your closing costs.

Closing costs are the laundry list of miscellaneous fees, charges, and other last-minute catches that have to be paid before your mortgage really is a done deal. If not handled right, they can cost you dearly—and, not incidentally, take all the fun out of buying a house.

The fact is that closing costs vary widely—often by thousands of dollars—and many of them are negotiable. Four of the most negotiable are application fees, appraisal fees, title fees, and title insurance premiums. **Don't be afraid to ask about them up front—and don't be afraid to question them.** Remember, you are not going to get a better deal unless you ask for a better deal at the time of application—waiting until closing will be too late.

APPLICATION FEES

To protect against the potential waste of their time, many lenders charge would-be borrowers an "application fee" that ranges from $50 (the price of pulling your credit score) to $395. Certainly, they are entitled to do so. But if a mortgage does close, many will agree to waive the fee. However much yours is, make sure to ask what it represents. In some cases, it will include the cost of the appraisal and credit report, in which case you're not likely to get it back. But if it doesn't, you have every right to ask that it be refunded if and when your loan closes.

APPRAISAL FEES

The lender can and usually does insist that you have the house you want to buy valued by a professional appraiser of his choosing. This can lead to a take-it-or-leave-it situation when it comes to the appraisal. Still, given that these fees vary widely (from as little as $150 to as much as $750), if they are on the high side, ask why—and see if there is anything they can do to help you get a better deal. Most lenders will offer you at least three different appraisers to choose from.

TITLE FEES AND TITLE INSURANCE

A key part of any home purchase is what is called the title search, a check of the real estate records to make sure that the seller is the legal owner of the property and that there are no liens or other claims outstanding against it. Lenders not only require you to pay for this search, they also expect you to take out title insurance that protects you and the bank in case any disputes arise over who really owns the property. Most lenders recommend—and often insist—that you use a specific title company to conduct the search and a specific title insurance firm to provide the coverage. Nonetheless, the title fees and the title insurance premium— which can total several thousand dollars— may be negotiable. If the seller bought the property only a few years ago, you may be able to get his title company to drop its normal fees and instead charge you what is called the "reissue rate." This is a much cheaper rate that title companies can charge when they already know the property and, hence, don't need to do as much original research to verify ownership.

GET AN ADVANCE COMMITMENT FROM A LENDER

Knowing that good mortgage deals are out there isn't enough. You want to be sure that one of them has your name on it—literally. This means getting a lender to give you an advance commitment for a particular mortgage at a particular rate before you even start looking for a house. With this kind of commitment in your pocket, you can begin your search secure in the knowledge that if and when you find a house you want to buy, you will be able to borrow the money you'll need on terms you can afford.

There are two types of commitments that lenders offer would-be homebuyers. One is called a "pre-qualification" and the other is called a "pre-approval." They may sound similar, but believe me—there's a huge difference between them.

"PRE-QUALIFIED" VS. "PRE-APPROVED"—THE CHOICE IS CLEAR

A "pre-qual" (as most professionals refer to it) is based on an informal review of your financial situation. The lender may ask you a series of basic financial questions (without requiring any written verification) and, based on your answers, give you an estimate of how much he thinks you'll be able to borrow. If you want, he will put this in writing, in what's generally known as a "pre-qual letter." You can then go out and look at real estate knowing that the lender "thinks" you should be able to get a loan for whatever amount he put in the letter. The entire pre-qualification process can take as little as 15 minutes. It's a snap.

Unfortunately, like most things that are so easy, it comes with a catch. The "pre-qual letter" is nothing more than a good-faith estimate by the lender—which is to say it's not binding. This means you can find a home, make an offer, have it accepted, and then hear from the lender, after he has completed a formal investigation of your credit record (which, among other things, will require you to document all the financial information you previously provided verbally), "Oops, sorry, but now that we've seen all your financials, we can't provide you with the loan we thought we could."

This sort of thing happens all the time. That's why some experts say that pre-quals are not worth the paper they're printed on— and why most smart real estate agents these days insist that buyers get pre-approved for a mortgage, rather than just pre-qualified. Pre-approval carries weight because it means the lender has made a real commitment to loan you the money.

GETTING PRE-APPROVED FOR A LOAN TAKES MORE TIME, BUT IT'S WORTH IT

Where pre-qualification is quick and informal, pre-approval is serious and time-consuming.

When you ask a lender to pre-approve you for a mortgage, you are asking him to formally review your financial situation, decide whether you are creditworthy, and then, assuming you are, commit to lending you a certain amount of money on particular terms, subject only to your finding an appropriate property.

To do all this, the lender will pull your credit report and score and study your credit history to see whether you can be trusted to pay your bills on time. Depending on your credit score, the lender may want to verify both your current income and your income history. They may want to see copies of your tax returns for the last three years, especially if you are self-employed, and they will want to see a verified list of all your assets and liabilities. They may ask you for copies of your bank statements (often going back three to six months). In essence, the lender is looking for as clear and accurate a picture as they can get of your financial situation. Can you afford the loan you want? Is it a safe bet that you would pay it back on time?

Because this review is so thorough, it may take several days to complete. But once it's done, you'll have a real commitment that you can literally bank on.

I strongly recommend that you take the time NOW—before you start looking at homes—to work with your mortgage advisor to get pre-approved by a lender. You're going to have to do this work eventually when you find a home you want to buy. So why put it off? It's so much smarter—and safer—to do it **before** you spend hours, days, or maybe months looking at real estate.

APPLYING FOR A MORTGAGE IS EASIER THAN YOU THINK

The great news about mortgages in the twenty-first century is that it's NEVER been easier to get approved for one. That's because lenders no longer worry as much as they used to about the risks involved in lending money to homebuyers. Why? Because these days, even lenders who continue to service their customers' loans reduce their risk by packaging the mortgages they make with a lot of other mortgages into what are called mortgage-backed securities and selling them to investors in the financial markets.

This may sound a little complicated, but it's terrific for would-be homeowners, since it has led to both huge growth and huge competition in the mortgage-lending industry.

WHAT THE BANK IS WILLING TO LEND VS. WHAT YOU CAN AFFORD TO BORROW

If you have followed all the advice here so far, you may be pre-approved for a loan. But is it a smart one?

Most mortgage lenders work hard to come up with a smart loan—one that will be profitable for them as well as manageable for you. But at the end of the day, if they get it wrong and let you borrow more than you can really handle, it's not just their problem. It's yours as well.

With this in mind, you should generally assume that **the amount the bank or mortgage company is willing to loan you is more than you should borrow**. In the scramble for business, lenders have grown more willing to loan more money to more people with shakier credit. This may sound nice, but as government regulators see it, too many lenders have been making too many imprudent mortgage loans. So keep in mind the guidelines I laid out in Chapter

Three. The estimated cost of your monthly mortgage payment plus your other regular housing costs (like property taxes and insurance) should be somewhere between 29 percent and 41 percent of your gross income—exactly where depends on how robust your financial health happens to be.

And don't fool around with this. Do the math. Be realistic about your situation. Don't pretend you're in better shape than you really are. Look closely at the estimated mortgage costs and at how they compare to what the guidelines say you should be spending. If you're not sure how to go about figuring this out, there are plenty of online calculators that will help you crunch these numbers—including a "Homeowner Affordability Calculator" on my web site at **www.finishrich. com/homeowner** that will help you determine how much you can really afford.

PUT ON YOUR WALKING SHOES—IT'S TIME TO START LOOKING AT HOUSES

Now that you've checked—and, if necessary, corrected—your credit score, found yourself a mortgage, negotiated a great deal, and gotten yourself pre-approved, there's no reason to put it off any longer. You're fully prepared to go out and start shopping for a home!

In the next chapter, I'll guide you through my simple 12-step action plan to finding and buying a home.

AUTOMATIC MILLIONAIRE HOMEOWNER ACTION STEPS

Reviewing the actions we laid out in this chapter, here's what you should be doing right now to find yourself the best deal you can on a mortgage and get yourself pre-approved by a lender.

❑ Look in the newspapers and online to see what kind of mortgage deals are available.

❑ Get copies of your credit score and credit reports and arrange to correct any errors you find.

❑ Work with your mortgage advisor to get yourself pre-approved (NOT pre-qualified) for a mortgage.

❑ Negotiate your fees and closing costs to save yourself money.

❑ Go to **www.finishrich.com/ homeowner/chaptersix** to listen to the free audio supplement to this chapter.

CHAPTER SEVEN

FIND YOURSELF
A HOME
THE SMART WAY

You've got a budget and you've been pre-approved for a mortgage. Now you're ready to go out and start shopping for houses.

As I said before, one of the keys to becoming an **Automatic Millionaire Home-owner** is realizing that when you purchase a home, you are getting more than just a place to live in. You are also making an investment that can become the foundation for your financial security.

Think about John and Lucy Martin. They weren't "super investors." They were—and are—normal people who earned a normal income, bought a few homes over the years, and used the equity they built up in those homes to leverage their way to real wealth.

You can do just what the Martins did. It may take you a decade or two . . . or three. But over time, you can buy homes, live well, and—if you act intelligently and deliberately —make some serious money. It's not always easy to do—but it is definitely doable.

Here's how to get started.

STEP ONE: MEET WITH A REAL ESTATE AGENT

One of the first things John and Lucy Martin did when they decided to look for a home was to call a real estate agent. They found their agent through the mortgage coach they met at their local bank. You may be able to get a qualified referral from the advisor who helps you with your mortgage. A great real estate agent can make the entire process of home-buying faster, easier, and more profitable. In fact, finding one is so important that I've dedicated an entire chapter to the subject. It follows this one. Read it carefully and make sure to listen to the amazing interview I offer online at **www.finishrich.com/homeowner** on this topic.

> **STEP TWO: IF YOU'RE RENTING A HOUSE OR CONDO, ASK YOUR LANDLORD IF HE'S INTERESTED IN SELLING**

Here's something that very few people consider. If you're a renter, and you happen to be renting a house or a condo that you really like, ask your landlord if he would consider selling it to you.

How likely is it that he will? Unless you ask—**you'll never know.** Maybe he needs the money. Maybe he's getting divorced. Maybe his kids are about to go to college or he wants to start his own business. Who knows? The only way you can find out is to ask!

The advantage of doing this is that you can negotiate a price without competition, your landlord doesn't have to pay a commission to a real estate agent (which could make him more willing to do a deal—and maybe even pass along some of his savings to you), and it won't cost you a penny to move.

STEP THREE: FIGURE OUT WHAT KIND OF PLACE YOU WANT TO LIVE IN

So you called your landlord and he or she won't sell. Or maybe you don't like where you currently live enough to want to buy it.

That's fine. It just means it's now time to go out and start looking at new places.

The question is, what type of home do you want? Before you start looking, you need to figure out what you're looking for. Do you want a detached house with a nice little yard? Or would you rather live in a condo with a pool, a gym, and maybe a doorman? Are you a fixer-upper type who likes hanging out in a hardware store, spending your weekends on do-it-yourself projects? Or would you rather buy a brand-new home in a brand-new development where everything is taken care of in advance right down to the carpets?

Before you go any further, you need to ask yourself some basic questions—and answer them as honestly as you can.

12 QUESTIONS YOU NEED TO ASK YOURSELF BEFORE YOU START LOOKING AT HOMES

1. Do I want a detached house, a townhouse, or a condo?
2. Am I willing to work on home-improvement projects after I buy?
3. Do I have the skills and motivation to make smart improvements?
4. Do I have the time and cash it will take to make improvements?
5. How many bedrooms and bathrooms do I want—and how many do I really need?
6. Do I want a garage?

7. Do I want a yard or pool?
8. Do I care about the school system?
9. Do I plan to be in the home for a long time, or will this be a short-term purchase?
10. Am I willing to commute—and if so, how far?
11. Do I need to have convenient access to public transportation?
12. Am I looking at this home as a place to live or simply as an investment that I will sell or rent as quickly as possible?

At this point, it may be hard to be certain of all the answers. Just do your best with what you know now. Believe me, taking ten minutes to really consider these questions can wind up saving you a lot of time and frustration later on.

When I first got out of school, I bought a home with my best friend Andrew for $220,000. It was a three-bedroom, two-bath house in the suburbs that needed a lot of work. We were young, and we regarded the house as an investment. We figured we'd live in it for a year, then rent it out and move on to the next property.

As it turned out, what we thought would be only a few months of fix-up work ("just a little paint, some new floors and carpets") actually took us more than a year. Because we didn't have much money, we did most of it ourselves (including tiling the kitchen). That first year it seemed all we did after putting in 70-hour weeks at our regular jobs was work on the house. For two guys in their early twenties, this wasn't exactly how we wanted to be spending our weekends.

In the end, the experience taught us a ton about buying real estate. For one thing, I learned that I was definitely not a fixer-upper kind of guy. I also found out I hated living in the suburbs.

The point is that you sometimes don't know what you like or don't like until after you buy. And that's okay. If life is about anything, it's about learning. All the same, you should do your best now to really think about these questions.

STEP FOUR: DECIDE WHERE YOU'RE GOING TO LOOK—AND THEN START LOOKING

You can't buy what you don't see. This means being disciplined and adjusting your expectations to match your means. Remember John and Lucy Martin's story. They wanted to be near the base, but the neighborhoods nearby didn't have any houses in their price range. Still, they really wanted to become homeowners. So rather than doing what many people in their situation do— which is to give up and rationalize continuing to rent—they opened their minds to the possibility of living in a less expensive neighborhood.

As a result, they began looking in an area that wasn't their ideal neighborhood—at homes that weren't their dream homes. They weren't thrilled at having to lower their sights, but they were determined—and their discipline paid off for them in the long run.

SPEND YOUR WEEKEND GOING TO OPEN HOUSES

One of the most common techniques real estate agents use to sell a property is to hold an open house—that is, to open the place to the public for several hours (usually on a Saturday or Sunday) during which anyone who is interested can drop by and check it out. You can usually find a listing of open houses—complete with times, addresses, and a short description of the property—in the weekend real estate section of your local newspaper.

So this weekend, check the open-house listings, make a list of the ones in your price range, then get in your car and go look at them. In a matter of hours, you'll be able to see as many as a dozen properties and get a real sense of what's out there that you can afford.

GET A MAP, DRAW A CIRCLE, AND CREATE YOUR TARGET MARKET

You don't have to travel all over the world to find yourself a home. Just draw a circle on a map that covers an area within an hour's drive from where you live. I promise you, somewhere within that circle you are going to find a home in your price range.

Now, like the Martins' first place, that home may not be ideally located. Their friends gave them a hard time about moving off the base, and the neighborhood they could afford was twenty minutes farther out than they wanted to be. But the schools were good, and if that's what it took for them to become homeowners, then that's what they were going to do.

The bottom line is that you have to start somewhere.

IF YOU LIVE IN A CITY, TRY THE FIVE-MILE RULE

If you live in a city, you may not have to go so far afield. Just draw a five-mile circle around where you live. In an urban area, a circle that size will probably cover so much real estate that you'll be able to find a place you like and can afford within ten minutes of your current home.

New York is a classic example of this. Talk to virtually anyone under the age of 35 and unless they are making a fortune, they'll tell you they can't afford to buy a home in Manhattan. Of course they can't. The average price of a Manhattan apartment is currently more than $1 million! Can you believe that?

But Manhattan isn't the only place to live in New York. Get on the train and go just five stops out of the borough (a trip that shouldn't take you much more than ten minutes or so), and you'll find brand new homes starting at $300,000 in areas like Williamsburg in Brooklyn and Sunnyside in Queens. The smart people who took this train ride out of Manhattan a few years ago and bought in these areas have made a fortune because their new neighborhoods are now booming. Why? Because affordable neighborhoods are in huge demand!

Consider what's happened in Oakland, California. In the 1990s, you couldn't give away real estate in Oakland. I know because I worked there at the time. The place was down and out, not to mention crime-ridden. Then again, it was just a ten-minute drive from San

Francisco. Fast forward a decade, and now Oakland is booming. Between 2000 and 2005, housing prices in Oakland soared by more than 144 percent. The city is now one of the hottest real estate markets in the country.

This is a really important point. Neighborhoods that are farther out or older or even somewhat dangerous may not be "hot" right now, but this can change quickly as people like you who can't afford the trendy areas begin to move in.

STEP FIVE: USE THE INTERNET TO DO YOUR OWN RESEARCH

Because of the Internet, looking for real estate is easier than ever. These days, you can spend a couple of hours online and gather information about potential neighborhoods that would have taken you months to assemble ten years ago.

The place where I'd start is Google (**www.google.com**), one of the most powerful search engines around. Just type in the name of the area you're interested in and add the words "real estate." Google will do the rest. You'll be amazed how much information you can accumulate without ever leaving your house.

Of course, while Google is a good place to start, it's not the only Internet resource you should use. There are countless real estate web sites loaded with information about what's available, where, and for how much. Most of these are commercial sites run by the big national real estate firms, but, hey—you're looking to buy a house, and that's what they are selling.

MY FAVORITE REAL ESTATE WEB SITES

realestate.yahoo.com	www.century21.com
www.coldwellbanker.com	www.homefair.com
www.homes.com	www.homestore.com
www.realestate.com	www.reals.com
www.realtor.com	www.remax.com

STEP SIX: **CONSIDER BUYING IN NEW DEVELOPMENTS**

As I write this, the market for new homes is absolutely booming. I can literally open a local newspaper in just about any community anywhere in the country and find a bunch of ads for new housing developments.

There are many exciting advantages to buying in one of these new developments. Here are six.

ADVANTAGE NO. 1: NEW HAS WHAT THE MARKET DEMANDS

There really isn't anything like a new home or condo. Providing the builder did his job right, you get a brand new place with all the most popular amenities. Big or small, house or apartment, if it's new, chances are it's been designed with an eye toward curb appeal. That's real estate jargon for the flashy features that make potential buyers want to whip out their checkbooks—things like bigger kitchens, more open space, larger closets, and bigger master baths.

This is important because when it comes time to sell (especially if you plan to do so within five years), you want to be offering a property that other people will find desirable.

ADVANTAGE NO. 2:
EVERYTHING WORKS

When you buy a new home, everything works—and if something doesn't, it's usually covered by a warranty that protects you for a least a year. Sure, you can always buy a homeowners policy to cover repairs in an older home, but your chances of having problems in an older property are much higher than in a new property, and even if your bills are covered, you don't need the hassle. Moreover, if the house is more than 20 years old, the problems—with plumbing, wiring, termites, foundations, etc.— can be endless. A new property isn't likely to have any of these woes.

ADVANTAGE NO. 3: DEVELOPERS CAN HELP YOU WITH FINANCING

In order to make the process of purchasing a home easier, many major homebuilders will help you with the financing—in some cases offering mortgages with down payments as small as just $1,000, in others offering interest rates fixed at 2 percent for the first year, 3 percent for the second year, and 4 percent for the third year, after which the rate adjusts. How can they do this? Well, some of the larger developers now own their own mortgage companies—and providing attractive financing helps them sell their homes faster. It's smart business for them, and it makes things easier for you.

ADVANTAGE NO. 4: NEW DEVELOPMENTS ARE GENERALLY LOCATED WHERE PEOPLE ARE MOVING TO

More often than not, the most important decision a builder makes when he plans a housing development is how much he is willing to pay for the land. A smart developer will tell you that if he makes a good deal on the land, he can pretty much guarantee his profits on the rest of the project. This usually means avoiding relatively expensive land in areas where people are living now and buying inexpensive land in areas where people will eventually be moving to.

How do developers identify these soon-to-be-hot areas? They spend millions studying demographic trends and analyzing population movements. They look at where new roads are being built, where new freeways are being extended. Is there public transportation on the way? Is the city planning to build a new park in the area? Smart developers keep tabs on these sorts of things and buy up the land before regular people (like you and me) have a clue that anything is going on.

The point is that when you buy in a new development, especially if you buy from one of the bigger developers, you get the benefit of all the demographic research they've done

BEWARE OF "SIZZLING" MARKETS

All these advantages are great, but you still need to do your homework. Not only are there plenty of fly-by-night developers looking to prey on unwary consumers, there are also some areas that many experts worry are being over-developed—most notably, Miami and Las Vegas. If you buy in a sizzling market at the wrong time, you can lose your shirt.

As I write this, there are some 60,000 condos under construction, approved for construction, or at some stage in the permit process in Miami and an estimated 40,000 in Las Vegas—half of which, experts estimate, are being bought by speculators who hope to flip them for a profit. My guess is that in a few years many of the condos in these markets will end up in foreclosure when the people who bought them find they can't sell them for a profit or rent them for enough money to cover their mortgage payments.

But guess what? This bad news for speculators could be good news for you. Once the bubbles burst in some of these crazy markets, you may find some amazing properties selling for 50 percent less than they did in 2005, creating some great opportunities to buy relatively new homes or condos at foreclosure prices.

to identify an area that's about to experience a boom. In other words, you often get in on the ground floor of what could be the next hot new area where homeowners are likely to enjoy major price appreciation.

ADVANTAGE NO. 5: NEW IS OFTEN EASIER TO SELL THAN OLD

Sooner or later (and probably sooner), you will be selling your home. If you bought new, chances are your property will still be in good condition and, therefore, you won't have to spend a bunch of money to get it in shape to sell. What's more, if you're in a new development, there's likely to be built-in demand from potential buyers who missed out on the first phase and now really want to get in.

ADVANTAGE NO. 6: NEW IS OFTEN
EASIER TO RENT

In Chapter Ten, we will look at how to go from simply owning the home you live in to buying additional homes that you may rent out. For now, suffice it to say that if you are considering someday renting the home you are about to buy, you should be aware that it's usually a lot easier to rent a new home than a old one. What's more, you're bound to experience far fewer maintenance hassles.

> ### STEP SEVEN:
> ### CONSIDER BUYING A FIXER-UPPER

I just gave you six reasons why buying a new house can be a great investment. But that doesn't mean you should rule out buying an older one.

As I mentioned, my first experience with homebuying taught me I wasn't a fixer-up kind of guy. But that's me. Many people— including many of my clients and students —have made fortunes fixing up homes (and had a lot of fun at the same time).

The obvious advantage to buying a fixer-upper is that it's going to be less expensive than a house that's in great shape. Another advantage is that after you've fixed it up, you may be able to turn around and sell it for a nice profit. This is how many people get started in real estate investing, and it's a great business for those who don't want to be landlords and deal with tenants.

One of my favorite examples of a successful fixer-upper comes from a former client of mine named Daryl. A petroleum engineer by trade, he retired from Chevron at age 60 and looked forward to playing golf all day, every day.

Within six months, he was bored silly. And before long, he was driving his wife, Vicki, crazy. Then one day he stumbled upon an open house for a place that "needed work."

The next morning he turned up at my office with a plan. "The house is going for $350,000," he told me. "I think it needs about $45,000 worth of renovations. What do you think about me buying this place and fixing it up? Based on what the neighborhood is like and what homes there are going for, I bet I could sell it for about $500,000."

I trusted Daryl's estimate because he had lived in the neighborhood for 20 years. But I still had a question. "Who's going to do the work?" I asked.

"Vicki and I will. We think it will be fun."

I told Daryl my story of how much "fun" I'd had fixing up my house, but Daryl wasn't put off. "This is something I've always wanted to do," he said. "We're gonna give it a shot."

Long story short, Daryl and Vicki not only did most of the work themselves, but they got it done in less than four months, after which they resold the property for $485,000. That was a little less than the $500,000 Daryl had hoped to get for the place, and their fix-up costs totaled around $55,000, about 20 percent more than Daryl originally figured. Still, after paying the real-estate agent's commission on the sale, they still managed to clear more than $50,000 in profit!

After that, Daryl was hooked. He's now gone the fixer-upper route four times in the last six years. And he's not only having fun, he's also making money—so much that he hasn't had to tap into his retirement nest egg.

HOW TO EVALUATE A FIXER-UPPER

Fixer-uppers come in two basic categories: There are cosmetic fixer-uppers and then there are structural fixer-uppers.

A cosmetic fixer upper is a home that merely needs to be freshened up. The work required may be as simple as buffing out hardwood floors or clearing the yard and laying down new sod. At most, it may involve putting new fronts on the kitchen cabinets. Cosmetic fixes are almost always cheaper and easier to do than structural ones.

Structural fixes are exactly what they sound like. They involve the "big stuff," such as roofing, wiring, plumbing, or foundations, which generally means a lot of work and a good-size bill. The good news is that problems like these can be so expensive or difficult to fix that you can almost always get a really good deal on houses that suffer from them.

In either case, before you take on a fixer-upper, make sure you know the facts. Get at least three first-rate contractors to give you estimates of what they think the work will cost and how long it will take. Then add 50 percent and ask yourself if you really have the time and money to take on the project.

3 SECRETS TO SUCCESSFUL FIXER-UPPERS

1. **Don't buy a fixer-upper in a neighborhood filled with them.** The secret to making real money in this game is to buy a fixer-upper in the nicest area you can afford. You want a property that's at the low end of prices in the neighborhood, not the high end. To put it bluntly, it should be the worst house on the best block.

2. **Ask your lender about special home-improvement loans.** Some companies now offer what are called "renovation loans" or "purchase and renovate loans" —mortgages that finance both the purchase of a house and the cost of fixing it up.

3. **Make sure you leave yourself room for upside!** Don't expect to sell a fixer-upper for a profit unless you're able to buy it at a bargain price. What this means is that you should only consider fixer-upper properties that are at least 20 percent below prevailing market prices.

STEP EIGHT: **CONSIDER BUYING A TWO-FAMILY HOME**

This is a great option for would-be homebuyers whose income is erratic, uncertain, or just too small to cover the costs of owning a home. The idea is simple: You live in one of the apartments, rent out the other one—and use the proceeds to cover part or all of your mortgage payments and other expenses.

You may think, "I could never afford a two-family home." But you might be wrong. Often, the rent from one unit can help you pay for a huge portion of your mortgage. I have friends who live in the upper level of a duplex they own, and the rent they get from the lower unit practically covers their monthly payment for the entire building. In other words, they almost live for free.

When you buy a two-family home with the idea of renting out one of the units, what counts is the cash flow it can generate. As long as you can charge enough rent to cover your expenses, it doesn't really matter what the total costs are.

What does matter is being comfortable with the responsibilities that go along with being a landlord. You're the one who is going to be called when a pipe breaks at two in the morning. That said, dealing with tenants doesn't have to be a nightmare. The trick is being selective about who you rent to. There are entire books written about just this issue. But the long and the short of it is that you can't discriminate based on race, religion, age, or gender. What you can do is make sure that your potential renter is reliable. You can check their credit history (get their permission and have them pay for it) and request references from former landlords and current employers. Best of all, you can hire a property management company to do all of this work for you.

STEP NINE: FIND OUT WHAT COMPARABLE PROPERTIES ARE SELLING FOR

One of the things that can make buying real estate complicated is that it's often hard to figure out what a particular house is really worth.

There's only one way to know for sure. That's to "run the comps"—to research what comparable houses in the same neighborhood have been selling for. Any good real estate agent will be able to do this for you at no cost, and in recent years a number of web sites have sprung up that allow you to do it for yourself. One of the best is **www. homesmartreports.com,** which charges $25 for a solid analysis of sales trends in any given neighborhood that takes into account the number of foreclosures as well as how many recent sales have been "fix and flips." Less detailed "comps" are available for free from **www.domania.com** and **www.home gain.com** and for $6.95 from **www.equi fax.com**.

Most experts recommend you look back between 90 to 180 days. But it really depends on the market. Real estate is local. Some markets are so hot that you need to gauge the most recent comps possible. Other areas are so slow that you may have to research property sales going back more than a year to get a feeling for the market.

You should run the comps even if you know the neighborhood. Thinking you know what prices are and actually knowing them are two different things. Your purchase decision should be based on hard facts, not hunches.

STEP TEN: MAKE AN OFFER

If you're not scared when you make an offer on a home, you are definitely the exception, not the rule. Most people get really nervous when they make an offer on a property. There are so many factors to consider—and so much money at stake—that pulling the trigger can be downright nerve-wracking.

Having purchased three properties in the last three years, I can tell you that it does get easier the more you do it. But that doesn't mean it's ever really easy.

I certainly understand what it is like to freeze up and not be able to make a decision. Back in the mid-1990s, I found myself unable to pull the trigger for nearly four years!

It began when my friend Andrew and I were finally able to rent out the suburban fixer-upper we owned for enough money to cover our mortgage. I was more than ready to move into San Francisco, but I wasn't comfortable yet with the prices there, so I rented an apartment in the Marina district for $1,250 a month. Before long, I realized renting was silly, and I asked my landlord if she would be interested in selling her building to me. It was a small building, consisting of just two one-bedroom apartments, and I figured it couldn't be that expensive.

As it turned out, my landlord was interested in selling, but she wanted $500,000 for the building. My little apartment, she said, was worth $250,000.

I thought that was crazy. So instead of buying, I became a "professional open house looker" on weekends. Over the next few months, I looked and looked and looked at homes in the Marina. Pretty soon, I was very knowledgeable about the local real estate market. I knew what was selling and what wasn't. I could tell almost immediately if a house was priced right. I also got to know the local real estate agents, because I talked to them at the open houses I visited.

Unfortunately, I didn't make any offers. Two years passed, and now my apartment, which I could have bought for $250,000 when I first moved in, was now worth closer to $350,000. The building that I had been offered for $500,000 was now worth around $750,000!

Had I learned anything?

Of course not. Once again, I thought it was crazy. "The market has to drop!" I told myself, and did nothing.

KNOWLEDGE WITHOUT OFFERS COSTS MONEY

By the time I bought, I had wasted four years looking! As a result, I wound up paying $640,000 for a two-bedroom condo that I probably could have bought for about $300,000 when I first moved to the Marina. Of course, I was able to make a nice profit when I sold it for $900,000 less than four years later. But if I'd bought it when I should have, I would have made twice as much.

My paralysis cost me a lot of money. If I had to do it all over again, I would have run the comps and made an offer the moment my landlord told me she was willing to sell.

Learn from my lesson. Follow the steps

I've laid out in this chapter and start looking at properties. Spend a few weekends (maybe even a month) going to open houses. But then STOP LOOKING AND MAKE AN OFFER.

The biggest mistakes I've made in real estate haven't been what I've bought—but what I didn't buy when I had the chance. It's the offers you don't make that wind up costing you the most money.

STEP ELEVEN:
BE PREPARED TO CLOSE

When you make that offer on a house and then get the great news that it's been accepted, you're not home free. You still have to close on the purchase, and this can be a complicated process that takes weeks if not months. Here are four things you can do to make sure the closing process goes as smoothly and quickly as possible. Your real estate agent should be able to assist you with all of these.

1. **Order up a home inspection—and attend it yourself.** Unless you are purchasing a new, custom-built property, you should never close on a house without having it first checked out by a professional home inspector. You should be able to get a referral from your real estate agent or your mortgage advisor—preferably from both. And make sure he is either a member of the American Society of Home Inspectors (**www.ashi.org**) or the National Institute of Building Inspectors (**www.nibi.com**). A properly performed home inspection is essential, since it will uncover any serious problems involving structural issues, leaks, faulty appliances, electrical and plumbing woes, and so on. (You might also consider ordering up a termite inspection and, if the property has water tanks or a well, a water inspection, too.) Although a professional inspector will provide you with a written report of his findings, don't just wait for him to

submit it. Show up at the house and personally watch him conduct the inspection. If you have a real estate agent (and you should), make sure he or she also attends. It would be nice to think all home inspectors are created equal, but they are not. **Chances are yours will do a better job if he knows you are looking over his shoulder.**

2. **Arrange to get homeowners insurance.** Your lender will probably require you to have homeowners coverage before you close. But whether or not he does, get going on this now. The homeowners policy should protect you from loss due to fire, weather damage, burglary, and so on. If you live in an earthquake or flood zone, you may need a separate policy to cover that possibility. If you're buying a condo, find out what type of coverage the building has and what you'll need to get yourself.

WEB SITES TO HELP YOU FIND A GOOD DEAL ON INSURANCE	
EDUCATIONAL SITES	**SHOPPING SITES**
www.consumerfed.org	www.allquotesinsurance.com
www.insurance.info	www.homeownerswiz.com
www.nclnet.org	www.homesite.com
www.pueblo.gsa.gov	www.netquote.com

3. **Alert your lender.** Even though you've been pre-approved for a mortgage, that doesn't mean you can assume it's a done deal. For one thing, the lender has to confirm the value of the home you're buying. For another, there is all kinds of extremely important paperwork that must be done. The sooner your lender gets started processing all this, the sooner you will be able to close.

4. **Arrange to have the property appraised by a professional.** Aside from the home inspection, nothing is more essential to a home purchase—or more

likely to delay the closing—than a professional appraisal of the property's value. Since it can take weeks to get one done, work with your lender to get the appraisal going the moment your offer is accepted.

STEP TWELVE: GIVE YOURSELF A DEADLINE—AND PUT IT IN WRITING

I'm a big believer in "dreams with deadlines." If you really want to buy a home, then one of the most important things you can do to make that dream come true is to set a deadline for yourself.

On page 255 is what I call the **Automatic Millionaire Homeowner Promise.** Please get a pen and fill it out right now. This may seem silly, but trust me—I've seen firsthand how effective this kind of exercise can be to really get you moving.

There will be some people who read this book and complain that it's too late for them to buy a home, much less get rich in

THE AUTOMATIC MILLIONAIRE HOMEOWNER PROMISE

I, _____ (insert name), know I deserve to own a home, and I know I can do it.

I promise myself that I will get my mortgage pre-approved by _____ (insert date).

I hereby promise myself that starting on _____ (insert date), I will begin going to open houses.

I will make an offer on a property by no later than _____ (insert date).

I promise myself that I will be a homeowner by _____ (insert date).

Signed: _____

real estate. They will have bought this book to fulfill a dream, but they won't do anything with it.

Then there will be people who read it and then take action! Be one of them. Let others keep wishing and hoping. Become a doer who gets things done. And do it right now—this minute! **Make a commitment— and sign it!**

SO YOUR MORTGAGE HAS BEEN APPROVED: HOW TO SURVIVE THE CLOSING

It's always exciting when your mortgage advisor calls to say that the lender has checked out the house you want to buy and given your pre-approved mortgage the final and official okay. But don't break out the champagne just yet. There are a number of things you need to do to make sure your interests are fully protected.

To begin with, you should carefully review the terms of your new mortgage with your banker or broker. Are the term, the interest rate, and ALL the other conditions (such as rate caps, points, prepayment penalties, and so forth) exactly what you were told they would be? If not, insist on getting a full explanation of what has changed and why.

AVOID LAST-MINUTE SURPRISES BY UNDERSTANDING YOUR CLOSING COSTS AHEAD OF TIME

Hopefully, you negotiated your closing costs when you got pre-approved for your mortgage (go back and re-read the section beginning on page 205). Either way, by law, within three days after you have applied for a mortgage, a lender must provide you with a "good faith estimate" of what your closing costs are likely to be. Even better is to ask if the lender will **guarantee** a specific closing cost price. Most lenders won't do this, but some will. In any case, you have a legal right to see a preliminary version of what's called your HUD-1 form, which sets out in detail all the closing costs associated with your mortgage, at least one full day prior to your closing.

To give you an idea of what to expect—and what is fair—some typical settlement fees are listed on the next page.

ESTIMATED CLOSING COSTS

Closing costs vary depending on where you live. Below is a list of typical costs and price ranges. Estimates are based on a $150,000 home with a 20% down payment.

Cost	Price
Application fee (may include credit report fees)	$75–$300
Loan origination fee	1% to 1.5% of loan
Appraisal fee	$350–$700
Lender's inspection fee	$175–$350
Title search, lender's title insurance	$700–$900
Recording fees for deed, mortgage, city/county/state taxes	Up to 1.5% of loan
Settlement fees	$500–$1,000

Source: Federal Reserve Board

MAKE SURE YOU READ YOUR HUD-1 REPORT THOROUGHLY

As I just noted, the HUD-1 is an official, itemized statement that lists all of the costs of your mortgage (including closing costs, interest charges, property taxes, monthly payments, and so forth) along with a full amortization schedule. You are entitled to get a preliminary copy of this statement at least a full 24 hours before closing. Very few people know this or ask to see their HUD-1 ahead of time. Given how many unexpected costs often pop up literally at the last minute, not looking at your HUD-1 as early as possible—and reviewing it with both your lender and an attorney—is a huge mistake.

Believe me, you don't want to be looking at it for the first time in a title office just after being handed a three-inch-thick stack of contracts to sign. I recently closed on a commercial loan for an office condo I purchased—and reading my HUD-1 the night before enabled me to catch a serious error. My mortgage was supposed to be a 20-year loan with a 10-year balloon payment (meaning that while the payments were calculated as if I had 20 years to pay the loan back, it would actually come due in just 10 years). Instead, when reading the HUD-1, I saw that it indicated that the balloon payment was due in just five years. I immediately called my bank and my attorney, and they fixed the "typo" in minutes and apologized for not catching it. If I hadn't read the loan document closely the night before, I could have ended up with a different loan than the one I was promised—one that would have cost me thousands of dollars.

So make a point of asking for your HUD-1.

GREAT TIP: The Federal Reserve has prepared a really helpful pamphlet called **A Consumer's Guide to Mortgage Settlement Costs.** You can get it for free online by going to the Fed's web site at **www.federalreserve.gov**. Just click on "consumer information."

Congratulations! You now know how to find and buy yourself a home—the smart way. Next, I'm going to let you in on a secret to making this process even less stressful and more enjoyable.

AUTOMATIC MILLIONAIRE
HOMEOWNER ACTION STEPS

Reviewing the actions we laid out in this chapter, here's what you should be doing right now to find yourself a home to buy.

- ❏ Complete and sign The Automatic Millionaire Homeowner Promise.

- ❏ If you're renting, see if your landlord is willing to sell.

- ❏ Figure out what kind of home you want to buy.

- ❏ Create a target market and start going to open houses in that area.

- ❏ Consider new developments, fixer-uppers, or two-family homes.

- ❏ When you find a house you like, "run the comps" and make an offer!

- ❏ Notify your lender and prepare to close.

- ❏ Go to **www.finishrich.com/ homeowner/chapterseven** to listen to the free audio supplement to this chapter.

CHAPTER EIGHT

HOW TO HIRE A GREAT REAL ESTATE COACH

Let's be honest. Even with everything you've learned about becoming an Automatic Millionaire Homeowner, buying and selling homes can still be a stressful business. There's a lot to do and a lot to know.

Fortunately, there's a simple way to make the process easier and even enjoyable. What you need to do is get yourself a licensed professional real estate agent. A great real estate agent can be the coach you need to make your homebuying experience both enjoyable and profitable.

This is exactly what John and Lucy Martin did. Throughout it all, from the Martins' first starter home to their most recent dream house, real estate agents guided them along the path to smart homeownership—which ultimately led them to become Automatic Millionaire Homeowners. And real estate agents have done the same thing for me. Like the Martins, I've used real estate agents in every one of my real estate transactions, both buying and selling. The value these professionals have given me over the years has both saved and made me a fortune.

Now it's your turn. This chapter is designed to teach you what exactly a good real estate agent does and how to find a great one. It won't take you long to read, but it could make the difference between a journey that's fun and profitable and one that's stressful and unproductive.

8 IMPORTANT THINGS A GREAT REAL ESTATE AGENT CAN DO FOR YOU

Before I became a financial advisor, I was a real estate agent (specializing in commercial properties), and I've worked with real estate agents on all of my real estate transactions. I know personally how much they can help you. But I also know that not all real estate agents are created equal. As of this writing, there are roughly 2 million real estate agents in the United States, with more entering the profession every day. There are full-time agents and those who work part time. Many are great—but not all. So how do you find the one who can make you money and make your life easier during the homebuying process? Here's a list of things you should look for:

1. **A great real estate agent will listen to you carefully.** Great agents are great listeners. They have to be in order to really help you. When a great agent

meets with you for the first time, he or she will pepper you with questions to find out what you're looking for, what you really want, why you want it, and most important, what you think you can afford.

2. **A great real estate agent will help you figure out what you really can afford.** As I've discussed before, when it comes to buying a home, there is generally a big difference between what you think you can afford and what you REALLY can afford. If you haven't already followed my advice to get yourself pre-approved for a mortgage, the first thing a top-notch agent will do is help you determine approximately how much house you are realistically going to be able to buy. At the very least, he or she will run your numbers and at least give you a "ballpark" estimate of what your price range should be. She will know which developments accept low- or no-

down-payment financing and which developments insist on 20 percent. A great agent will also provide you with referrals to at least three bankers or brokers who can help you get pre-approved for an exact mortgage amount.

3. **A great real estate agent will save you time by narrowing your search.** Finding the right house in the right location at the right price is not easy. A great agent will help you figure out what exactly you are looking for—and then whittle down the possibilities to manageable proportions. Among other things, he or she will take advantage of what's called the Multiple Listing Service (or MLS), a searchable, computerized directory of what's for sale that is available only to licensed professionals. A great agent won't run you ragged (and waste your time) by dragging you around to countless properties. Rather, the agent will show you a selection on-

line, allowing you to narrow your choices before you actually hit the streets. He or she will then "tour you" to ones you've chosen—and keep track of what you like.

4. **A great real estate agent will educate you about the market.** Great real estate agents know more than simply what's for sale in a particular neighborhood. They know the neighborhood. They can tell you all about an area's history, what makes it special, and where they see the market there going. If you're looking at a new development, the agent can share with you what he or she knows about the developer's track record and plans for the future.

5. **A great real estate agent will help you determine what price to offer for a property you want to buy—and how to evaluate a purchase offer when you're selling.** Once you find something you like, you're going to have to

make an offer. If you're selling a property, you're going to have to decide whether to accept or reject the offers you receive. To make smart choices, you will need a lot of information quickly. A great agent will get you that information. Perhaps most important, he or she will "run comps" for you—provide you with an analysis of what comparable properties in the area have been selling for.

6. **A great real estate agent will show you ways to get more value from the property.** From the moment a great real estate agent first sees a property, he or she is thinking about what could be done to increase its value. Install new cabinets in the kitchen, pull up the rugs, redo the hardwood floors, take down this wall, knock out the back bedroom and add a master bath—great agents will look at property and immediately begin suggesting ways you could make it more attractive and valu-

able. They can also refer you to reliable contractors who can turn those suggestions into reality. And they can help you "stage" a home that you're getting ready to sell—in essence, setting up the home to look its best for potential buyers.

7. **A great real estate agent will hold your hand at closing.** The closing of a home purchase at the title office can often be a scary few hours. A good agent will make sure you are thoroughly prepared. Great agents go over the paperwork with you and your attorney, checking it for errors. They will also work closely with you and your mortgage banker or broker to make sure your loan looks like it should and that all the closing documents are in place.

8. **When you are selling a house, a great real estate agent will market the property aggressively.** When you decide to sell a house, a great agent will handle all the marketing efforts.

In addition to helping you ready the property for sale by "staging it," these efforts may include preparing sales brochures or flyers; running advertisements in newspapers, real estate magazines, and online; getting the property listed on the MLS; and holding open houses for both real estate agents and the public.

HOW IS A REAL ESTATE AGENT PAID?

Real estate agents are almost always paid by commission—meaning that when a sale closes, they get a percentage of the purchase price (usually 6 percent). In other words, if the house sells for $200,000, the buyer's agent and the seller's agent (also known as the listing agent) are entitled to a commission of $12,000. Generally speaking, they split the commission 50/50. This commission is usually deducted from the proceeds of the sale—which is to say, **it is paid by the seller.**

IF YOU'RE SELLING, KEEP IN MIND THAT COMMISSIONS MAY BE NEGOTIABLE

If you're looking for an agent to help you **sell** a property, keep in mind that depending on the market, commissions may be negotiable. Real estate agents often give discounts to sellers who plan to buy another home with the proceeds from the sale—on the assumption that they'll be handling the purchase as well. So if that's what you're doing, make sure to ask. Also, if the market is really hot and properties are flying, a real estate agent may be willing to discount their commission because they know the property will move quickly and not take a lot of time to sell. (On the other hand, if the market is slow or you insist on asking too high a price for your property, a smart real estate agent is not likely to give you a break.)

A discounted commission may drop the standard commission from 6 percent to 5.5 percent or even 5 percent. That may not sound like much, but if you can get a 6 percent fee cut to 5 percent, you'll save yourself $2,000 on the sale of a $200,000 home.

AND NOW THERE'S SOMETHING CALLED THE BONUS COMMISSION

When real estate sales slow or there is a glut of properties similar to your home on the market in your neighborhood, it may take longer to sell your home. A great way to get a property to stand out and sell faster is to offer your agent a bonus commission. Instead of the standard 6 percent, you might offer a commission of 7 percent or 8 percent—provided they can find a buyer for your house within a certain amount of time or willing to pay above a certain price. This is not unheard of—and it can work like a charm. In Manhattan, where I live, creative sellers are even offering agents plasma-screen televisions, trips to Hawaii, and (in a few cases) cars as incentives to sell their places fast and for higher prices.

Whatever the commission winds up being, you should know that your real estate agent usually doesn't get to keep all of it. They usually have to split some of the commission with the brokerage company they work for, and they also have to pay for the costs associated with marketing the property. The fact is that most real estate agents end up really earning their commission. It's not an easy business.

IT'S IMPORTANT TO KNOW WHOM YOUR AGENT REPRESENTS

It is not unheard of in the real estate business for the same agent to represent both the buyer and the seller in a property transaction. While this is not illegal, it is not something I would recommend, since when you're buying or selling a house, you want to be represented by someone who has your interests at heart and no one else's.

One way to make sure this is the case is

FREE AUDIO BONUS!

HOW TO HIRE A GREAT
REAL ESTATE AGENT

At the beginning of this chapter, I said you shouldn't hire just any real estate agent but a great one! What distinguishes many real estate agents who are serious about their careers is membership in the **National Association of Realtors (NAR).** This organization provides continuing education and conferences to help real estate agents stay informed and grow their skills so they can provide you with extra value. Most NAR members have a REALTOR® logo on their business card or letterhead.

For more information about real estate agents and Realtors®—and how to find a good one—you can listen to a powerful interview I did with NAR senior vice president and chief economist David Lereah. Just go to my web site at **www.finishrich.com** and visit the Automatic Millionaire Homeowner resource center. This interview is loaded with great tips—and it's my free gift to you! Also visit **www.realtor.com** for great information about how to find both a Realtor® and a home.

to get in writing up front that in any and all deals, your real estate agent will be representing you and you alone. If you're a buyer, you can do this with what is called a "buyer's agreement"—basically a contract in which the agent agrees that he or she will look out for your best interests and represents only you, not the seller.

In return, the agent may ask you to promise to work with him or her exclusively (as opposed to improving your odds of finding a good deal by working with several different agents at the same time). If you are willing to sign an exclusive buyer's agreement, I recommend limiting your commitment to no more than 60 days—30 would be even better because it will motivate your agent to work hard and fast for you.

THE TRICKY PART OF WHO WORKS FOR WHOM

Occasionally, a real estate agent will show you a house that is represented by another agent at his or her firm. If this is the case, and you decide to buy the property, the sales contract will more than likely include a line noting that your agent actually does not represent you but rather represents the seller.

In this case, you MUST get an attorney. Don't let "your" agent tell you not to worry about it. If you sign a contract that says your agent represents the seller, you have no protection legally. So get yourself an attorney who can look over the contract—to be sure your interests are protected.

THREE BASIC RULES FOR HIRING A GREAT REAL ESTATE AGENT

As with anything else, hiring a great real estate agent is a matter of common sense and good judgment. Follow these three basic rules and you shouldn't go wrong.

> ### RULE NO. 1:
> ### GET A RECOMMENDATION

When you're ready to hire a real estate agent, don't be shy. Ask your friends, relatives, coworkers, and neighbors who they used the last time they bought or sold a home. Your goal should be to get at least three referrals, so you can compare a number of real estate agents before you decide to work with one.

> ### RULE NO. 2:
> ### IF YOU CAN'T GET A REFERRAL
> ### TO AN AGENT YOU LIKE,
> ### DON'T GIVE UP

Referrals are great, but they are not essential. It may be a little more challenging, but it is definitely not impossible to find a good agent on your own. Unless you live in the middle of nowhere, I'll bet at least a half dozen real estate brokerage firms have local offices in your neighborhood. Call three of them, ask for the manager, and tell him or her that you're looking for an experienced agent who specializes in working with someone like you.

In addition to "cold calling" real estate agencies, you can also do a little investigating on your own. I'm a big believer in the idea that success leaves clues. If you are looking for a house in a specific neighborhood, an incredibly easy way to find a top agent is simply to drive around the area looking for "For Sale" signs in front yards. When you see one, write down the name of the agent on it, and make a note of whose name you see the most. The agent with the most listings is usually an expert on that neighborhood. That's the guy or gal you probably want.

RULE NO. 3:
INTERVIEW, INTERVIEW, INTERVIEW

Don't make assumptions or take someone else's word for it. Even if an agent looks great on paper (and even if he or she has been recommended by your oldest and best friend), don't decide to work with anyone until you've sat down and conducted a long, searching interview.

When you meet with a real estate agent, I highly recommend that you ask the following questions.

- How long have you been in the business?
- How long have you worked in this particular market?
- How many listings (properties for sale where you represent the seller) do you have?
- How many clients are you currently working with?
- How many deals did you do last year in the area I'm interested in?
- Why should I work with you rather than one of your competitors?
- What makes you a good real estate agent?
- What is your process—how do you work with your clients?
- Do you have a team or an assistant? Will I be working with them or with you?

- Can you give me the names of three clients you've worked with whose situation was similar to mine?

These questions can quickly weed out an agent who's not for you. When I first moved to New York, I was referred by a friend to an agent he really liked—but within minutes, I knew the agent wasn't right for me. How did I know that? When I asked him how many lofts he had sold or helped someone buy over the last year in the neighborhoods I was interested in, he said the answer was none! So I thanked him for his time—and continued my search for a top agent.

MAKE A COMMITMENT

You now know more about what real estate agents do than 90 percent of the people who will ever buy or sell a home. In short, you are ready to get going. So right now, this very minute, make a commitment to yourself to go out and interview a real estate agent.

My hunch is that in no time you'll have a fantastic real estate agent on your side acting as your advocate and coach to help you find the right home for you.

At this point, you know enough to find a terrific home, financed with a mortgage, that is the right fit for you. But there's more to being an Automatic Millionaire Homeowner than owning a home. In the next chapter, I'm going to share with you a really simple system called an automatic biweekly mortgage payment plan that could save you tens of thousands of dollars in interest payments (maybe more) and shave up to seven years off the time it will take you to pay off your mortgage.

AUTOMATIC MILLIONAIRE HOMEOWNER ACTION STEPS

Reviewing the actions we laid out in this chapter, here's what you should be doing right now to find a great real estate agent you can trust.

- ❏ Make a commitment to go out and find yourself a top real estate agent.

- ❏ Ask everyone you know who has ever bought or sold a home whether they would recommend the real estate agent they used.

- ❏ "Cold call" local real estate brokerages and research local sales to compile a list of agents worth considering.

- ❏ Schedule interviews with the top three prospects and make a decision.

- ❏ Visit **www.finishrich.com/homeowner** and listen to my interview with David Lereah of the National Association of Realtors on how to hire a great real estate agent.

❑ Go to **www.finishrich.com/ homeowner/chaptereight** to listen to the free audio supplement to this chapter.

CHAPTER NINE

MORTGAGE AUTOMATIC AND SAVE $106,000 ON YOUR HOME

One of the most valuable secrets I've learned from my Automatic Millionaire friends like John and Lucy Martin—as well as the original Automatic Millionaires, Jim and Sue McIntyre—is the power of paying your mortgage off early by splitting your monthly payment into two biweekly payments.

In **The Automatic Millionaire**, I laid out a simple system that any homeowner can use to pay off a 30-year mortgage as much as seven years early . . . **automatically**. I shared this message on **The Oprah Winfrey Show,** and viewers were simply blown away by how easy this was. After my appearance, our phones rang off the hook. "How can that be?" people wanted to know. "It can't be that easy to save so much money on a mortgage. What's the trick?"

Well, in truth, it's not a trick.

Think about it this way. The problem with a 30-year mortgage is that it's designed to make you spend 30 years paying it off! Say you buy a home with a $300,000 mortgage at 7 percent. If you take the full 30 years to pay it off, you will wind up actually giving the bank close to $720,000, since in addition to paying back the principal, you will also pay more than $418,000 in interest.

What's a better approach? Well, if you were to take that same mortgage and make the payments on a biweekly instead of a monthly schedule, you would cut the total payment time by seven years—and in the process save yourself $106,000 in interest payments.

Want to see how easy this is?

PAY YOUR MORTGAGE
FASTER—PAINLESSLY

Here's how it works. All you do is take the normal 30-year mortgage you have and instead of making the monthly payment the way you normally do, you split it down the middle and pay half every two weeks.

Say your mortgage payment is $2,000 a month. Under my biweekly plan, instead of sending a $2,000 check to your mortgage lender once every month, you would send him $1,000 every two weeks. At the beginning, paying $1,000 every two weeks probably won't feel any different than paying $2,000 once a month. But as anyone who's ever looked at a calendar could tell you, it's hardly the same thing. A month, after all, is a little longer than four weeks. And so what happens as a result of switching to a biweekly payment plan is that over the course of a year you gradually get further and further ahead in your payments, until by the end of the year you have paid the equivalent of not 12 but 13 monthly payments. Best of all, because it is so gradual, you will hardly feel the pinch.

The math is actually quite simple. A monthly mortgage payment of $2,000 amounts to $24,000 a year. But when you make a half payment every two weeks instead of a full one once a month, you end up making 26 half payments over the course of a year. That's 26 payments of $1,000—for a total of $26,000, or one extra month's worth of payments, painlessly.

WHAT COULD YOU DO WITH AN EXTRA $106,000?

The impact of that extra month's payment is awesome. Depending on your interest rate, you will end up paying off a 30-year mortgage somewhere between five and seven years early, and a 15-year mortgage three years early! You will be debt-free years ahead of schedule, saving you tens of thousands of dollars in interest payments over the life of your loan.

I'm not just making these figures up. Check out the amortization schedule that follows. It shows the difference between a monthly and a biweekly payment plan for a $300,000 30-year mortgage with an interest rate of 7 percent. The monthly pay-off schedule winds up incurring a total of $418,026.69 in interest charges over the life of the loan. The biweekly schedule, on the other hand, runs up just $311,876.19 in interest. In other words, switching to the biweekly plan will save you more than $106,000.

If you'd like to figure out how much you could save on your own mortgage, go online and visit my web site at **www.finishrich. com/calculators.** Then look under "Mortgages" and click "Get a biweekly mortgage plan." This will take you to the best free calculator I've found on the Internet. You can then plug in your own numbers and quickly see how much you could save by switching to a biweekly payment plan.

ALL IT TAKES IS TEN MINUTES

The great thing about switching to a biweekly payment plan is that it allows you to save money over the long run without refinancing or otherwise changing your mortgage. All it takes is one call.

That's because these days most mortgage lenders offer programs designed to totally automate the process I've just described. (At Wells Fargo, for example, it's called the Accelerated Ownership Plan; CitiBank calls its the BiWeekly Advantage Plan.) To enroll, all you need to do is phone your lender or go online to its web site. Many banks offer this service for free to customers who do all their banking with them. Those banks that don't offer this service usually refer you to an outside company that runs the program for them. These companies generally charge a set-up fee of between $200 and $400. In addition, there's a transfer charge of $2.50 to $6.95 that's assessed every time your money is moved from your checking account to your mortgage account.

A lot of companies now provide these ser-

MONTHLY PAYMENTS VS. BIWEEKLY PAYMENTS

Principal=**$300,000**   Interest Rate=**7.00%**
Term=**30** years

Monthly Payment:	Biweekly Payment:
$1,995.91	**$997.9**
Average Interest	Average Interest
$1,162.57 vs.	**$398.82**
Each Month	Each Biweekly Period
Total Interest: **$418,026.69**	Total Interest: **$311,876.19**

Year	Principal Balance (Monthly Payments)	Principal Balance (Biweekly Payments)
1	$296,952.57	$294,809.35
2	$293,684.84	$289,244.18
3	$290,180.89	$283,277.48
4	$286,423.64	$276,880.28
5	$282,394.77	$270,021.51
6	$278,074.66	$262,667.87
7	$273,442.24	$254,783.66
8	$268,474.95	$246,330.60
9	$263,148.57	$237,267.64
10	$257,437.15	$227,550.77
11	$251,312.85	$217,132.83
12	$244,745.82	$205,963.21
13	$237,704.06	$193,987.70
14	$230,153.25	$181,148.14
15	$222,056.60	$167,382.19
16	$213,374.63	$152,623.01
17	$204,065.05	$136,798.94

Year	Principal Balance (Monthly Payments)	Principal Balance (Biweekly Payments)
18	$194,082.48	$119,833.15
19	$183,378.26	$101,643.26
20	$171,900.23	$82,140.94
21	$159,592.46	$61,231.51
22	$146,394.96	$38,813.45
23	$132,243.41	$14,777.89
24	$117,068.84	$0
25	$100,797.31	$0
26	$83,349.50	$0
27	$64,640.39	$0
28	$44,578.79	$0
29	$23,066.94	$0
30	$0	$0
Result:	Paid off in 30 years	Paid off in 23 years

Source: Bankrate.com "Biweekly mortgage payment calculator"

vices. To be sure you're dealing with a reputable firm, you should probably use one that is referred to you by your mortgage company. Currently, one of the largest providers of this service is a company called PayMap, which you can visit at **www.pay map.com**.

WHY NOT DO IT YOURSELF?

Why spend hundreds of dollars on an outside firm when you could just as easily use your bank's online automatic bill-paying service to schedule biweekly mortgage payments for yourself? Unfortunately, it's not really that simple.

The problem is that if you split your monthly mortgage payment in half and send it in to your mortgage lender every two weeks yourself, the lender will simply send it back to you because they don't have the ability to apply a half payment unless you are set up for a biweekly mortgage payment plan.

WHAT YOU COULD DO FOR FREE

You could add 10 percent to your regular mortgage check each month and have the money applied toward the principal. Or you could make one extra payment at the end of the year and again have it go toward your

principal. But note that word "could." Let's
face it—some things are much easier said
than done. Just like most people won't save
if they don't make it automatic—**in the real
world, most people won't make extra
mortgage payments unless they make it
automatic.**

If you decide to do it yourself, my suggestion is that you add an extra 10 percent a
month toward your mortgage payment—
and make the payment automatic. Also,
make a point of asking your lender to make
sure that this extra payment is credited
toward your principal—and then check your
monthly statements to make sure they did it
correctly.

PENNY-WISE OR POUND-FOOLISH?

Some people will complain when they read
this about the cost of a biweekly payment
plan. They are missing the point. When all
is said and done, the cost of running a bi-

weekly payment plan shouldn't cost you more than $100 a year. For this modest expense (probably less than $2,500 over the life of the loan), you will save tens of thousands of dollars. In the example I provided earlier, the savings totaled more than $106,000. I've had readers tell me this one idea saved them more than twice that!

And a biweekly payment plan does more than allow you to pay off your home early. It also makes it easier to manage your money, since most of us get paid every two weeks. You'll be richer faster with a plan that makes your life easier. So consider it.

You're on your way to becoming an Automatic Millionaire Homeowner.

AUTOMATIC MILLIONAIRE HOMEOWNER ACTION STEPS

Reviewing the actions we laid out in this chapter, here's what you should be doing right now to save yourself thousands of dollars by setting up an Automatic Biweekly Mortgage Payment Plan.

❑ Check out the calculator at **www. finishrich.com** to see how much time and money you could save by paying off your mortgage biweekly.

❑ Call your lender to find out if it offers a biweekly payment plan.

❑ Sign up for the plan—or if your lender doesn't offer one, contact a service company such as PayMap to set up a biweekly plan of your own.

❑ Go to **www.finishrich.com/ homeowner/chapternine** to listen to the free audio supplement to this chapter.

CHAPTER TEN

FROM ORDINARY HOMEOWNER TO AUTOMATIC MILLIONAIRE HOMEOWNER

By now you know more about the fundamentals of buying a house than 90 percent of all homeowners. And for those of you who have already used this knowledge to buy yourself your first home—congratulations! You are well on your way to a lifetime of financial security. But it need not stop there. In this chapter, I will show you how you can turn your home—your little gold mine—into a gold rush!

The key to transforming yourself from an ordinary homeowner to an Automatic Millionaire Homeowner is to learn how to use your new home to build yet more wealth. Whether you already own your home or you are about to take the plunge, your model should be John and Lucy Martin, who used the equity in their first home as the foundation for a lifetime of financial security.

DOING IT AGAIN— ONLY BETTER

The single most important thing the Martins did after deciding to become homeowners was actually something they didn't do. THEY DIDN'T SELL THEIR FIRST HOME. This was also true of the original Automatic Millionaires, Jim and Sue McIntyre, whom I wrote about in **The Automatic Millionaire**. For both of these couples, this smart but not obvious decision wound up having a profound impact on their ability to accumulate wealth.

In both cases, after living in their first homes for a while and building up some equity, these perfectly ordinary people earning a perfectly ordinary income didn't simply sell out and buy a bigger house. Instead, they rented out their first home, used the rental income to cover the mortgage payments on it, and borrowed against the equity they'd built up to purchase a new home to live in.

To do this, they had to adopt what I call the Automatic Millionaire Homeowner Mindset. This is a different way of thinking about your house. Most people think of their house simply as a place to live in. The Martins and McIntyres thought of their homes as places to live in but also as **vehicles for building wealth**.

BIGGER IS NOT ALWAYS BETTER

The Martins and the McIntyres didn't do what most people do. Most people buy a starter house, and then, as their family grows, they sell it and use the proceeds to buy a bigger house. Usually much bigger. This leads to bigger mortgage payments. Usually much bigger. In most cases, it's why very few people ultimately own more than one house at a time.

How could the Martins, who never earned a big income, afford to own two houses at the same time? It's simple. Unlike most people, who are stuck paying off their big mortgages by themselves, the Martins had tenants—and the rent they paid—to help them build equity.

If you go back and reread the story of the Martins, you'll see that when they bought their first home, their initial priority was to focus on paying down their mortgage early. And when their home went up in value, they didn't rush to cash out so they could buy a bigger house.

Remember what John Martin told me about what he and his wife did when they were ready to buy a second home that could accommodate their growing family: He said they had to stretch to make the purchase, but they didn't stretch too much. "In fact," he said, "we actually stretched a little **less** than we could afford because we had decided not to sell our first house but, instead, to keep it and rent it out. So instead of cashing out completely, all we did was refinance the house just enough to pull out a down payment on our new place."

You can do the exact same thing. Here's how.

WILL YOUR HOME GENERATE POSITIVE CASH FLOW?

Often, you don't have to live in your home all that long before it's capable of generating positive cash flow. If the real estate market goes up over five years and homes become more expensive in your area, in most cases rents will go up also. There are exceptions to this rule because every market is different, but it's usually the case that if housing prices go up, so do rents.

Check right now to see if rents in your area are high enough to cover the costs you'd incur if you were to rent out your place. Pull out the local newspaper and look at the rental ads, or have a real estate agent who specializes in rentals come over and evaluate your home.

Keep in mind that figuring out how much it would cost you to turn your house into a rental property involves more than just adding up your current mortgage payment and your property tax bill. You also need to figure in maintenance (the cost of everything from fixing leaky faucets to replacing balky furnaces) as well as extra insurance premiums and an allowance for vacancies and bad debts.

If it turns out that it would indeed be possible for you to charge enough rent for your place to cover all these costs, you need to ask yourself an important question: Are you ready to get into the landlord business? If you are, it may be time to consider getting a tenant for your current house and buying another for yourself.

BEING A LANDLORD IS EASIER THAN YOU THINK

Keep in mind that renting out a home can be easier than you think. You can hire a real estate agent to list it and a property management company to manage it. (Your real estate agent should be able to recommend a management company. Figure on paying them between 6 percent and 12 percent of your rental income.) Or you can do it all yourself.

The point is that managing one rental home doesn't have to be a big deal—but it can lead to great wealth over time, as someone else pays off your mortgage. Moreover, as I mentioned earlier, if you ever decide to sell your rental property, you can avoid paying any taxes on the profits by making what's called a 1031 or Starker Exchange.

If becoming a landlord is such a good deal, why aren't lots of homeowners doing it? In fact, they are. Nearly one out of four homes purchased in 2004 was bought for investment purposes—a trend **USA Today** credited with "transforming many Americans into first-time landlords."

YOUR TENANTS CAN PAY YOU TWICE

In some cases, you may be able to rent out your first house for enough money to cover not only all the costs of owning the property but also to cover some or all of the mortgage on your second home. This is what happened with the Martins, and it's an option for me right now.

As I write this in 2005, housing prices in New York City are through the roof. Our loft is worth at least $1 million more than I paid for it three years ago. What's more, rents have gone up to the point where we could rent it out right now for about $5,000 more a month than it currently costs us in mortgage payments and other costs. That's $60,000 a year in positive cash flow. Not bad.

I'm also currently in the process of buying

a new condo in a building still under construction in the currently trendy Brooklyn neighborhood of Williamsburg. The price of this condo was $700,000, and it's already worth close to $1,000,000. When I close, I will probably make a cash down payment of around $140,000, or around 20 percent of the purchase price. Depending on the mortgage I get, my monthly payments will be between $3,000 and $5,000.

I had originally thought of this place as an investment property I could rent out. But if my wife and I wanted to, we could rent out our Tribeca loft now for enough to cover its mortgage **and** generate sufficient positive cash flow to pay the mortgage on the Williamsburg condo, and maybe the maintenance, taxes, and insurance as well—meaning we could basically live there for free.

This is what is so much fun about real estate. It gives you so many options.

YOU REALLY CAN DO THIS AND HERE'S HOW

You can read these examples and get skeptical or jealous or you can get going! I know you want to get going. With this in mind, let's look at four strategies you can use to build wealth through homeownership.

> ### STRATEGY NO. 1:
> ### USE YOUR HOME EQUITY TO BUY YOUR NEXT PROPERTY

The equity you have in your home is an asset. It belongs to you, not the bank. If you take out a $200,000 mortgage to buy a home for $250,000 and the property's value rises to $400,000, the $150,000 increase is yours, not the bank's. You've now got $200,000 in equity. You can use it or you can let it sit there. The choice is yours.

What you need to know about home equity is this: Right now, most people have more equity in their homes than they realize. Even with all those "no down payment" mortgages, interest-only loans, and overambitious purchases where people buy more house than they should, the huge run-up in real estate values since the mid-1990s has left most Americans with a ton of equity in their houses—more than $10 trillion, as of this writing. (Even as cautious an expert as legendary Federal Reserve Chairman Alan Greenspan called that "a sizable equity cushion" that would allow "the vast majority of homeowners . . . to absorb a potential decline in house prices" if the market cools off.) But most people really don't appreciate or make good use of all this equity they own.

So how should you think about your home equity? There are at least three different ways. All are sensible, but only one of them—the third—will lead to your becoming an Automatic Millionaire Homeowner.

1. **As the ultimate safety net.** If you don't want to do anything risky, you can look at your home equity as a kind of forced savings account. You can pay

off your mortgage early, as I suggested a few pages back, and when you're older, you'll be able to retire with no debt. Later, if you ever need money, there are a variety of ways to make use of all the equity you have accumulated. The point is that you have a safety net—and options.

2. **As collateral for a loan.** Another way to take advantage of the equity in your current home is to arrange what is called a home-equity loan, in which the bank agrees to lend you the cash value of your equity. You should shop this loan just the way you would a regular mortgage to make sure you get a competitive rate. Keep in mind that home equity rates are almost always higher than those for a standard mortgage, and they don't always lock (meaning the rate is variable). So there is more cost and risk involved. But the interest is tax-deductible, and it is usually a lot easier to get a home-equity

loan than to get a mortgage. You can use a home-equity loan for any reason— to pay for your kids' college, to start your own business, or to take a trip to Europe. But my recommendation is that you only use your equity to buy more assets, not to pay for daily living expenses, vacations, or credit card debt.

3. **As a stepping-stone to buy a second home.** This is how Automatic Millionaire Homeowners think about their home equity. You can see this mind-set at work in John and Lucy Martin's story. When they were ready to buy a second home, they did what is called a "cash-out refinance." It works like this: Say you bought a home with a $250,000 mortgage and the place is now worth $400,000. You could go to a bank or mortgage broker and refinance—that is, get a new mortgage to pay off the old one. Only now you would borrow not $250,000 but, say, $300,000. This would allow

you to pay off the existing $250,000
mortgage—and put $50,000 cash in
your pocket. You then take that
$50,000 and use it as a down payment
on another home for you to live in
while you rent out your first house. Of
course, you now owe more money
($300,000 instead of $250,000), and,
depending on what type of new mortgage you get, your monthly payments
may be higher—which is something
you need to factor in when you're calculating whether the rent you think
you can charge will cover all your
costs.

In John and Lucy's case, their $30,000
starter house (remember, this was back in
the 1960s) had increased in value to about
$45,000 when they felt ready to buy their
second home. They had already reduced
their original mortgage balance to just
$20,000, so they had no trouble getting a
new $40,000 mortgage that paid off the old
one and left them with enough cash

($20,000) for a 20 percent down payment on the $100,000 home they had decided to buy. Eventually they sold this second house—for $650,000—and moved to their dream home. By then, of course, they owned their first house free and clear. With the rent they earned from it over the years, they'd long since paid off its $40,000 mortgage and were now enjoying the positive cash flow it continued to generate—not to mention the phenomenal contribution to their net worth, as the house's value skyrocketed toward seven figures. They had become Automatic Millionaire Homeowners.

A GREAT EXAMPLE OF LEVERAGE

This is a classic example of how you can leverage your way to wealth. The Martins put $6,000 down on a starter home that within a few years was worth $45,000. (Keep in mind that even though the price of that house was $30,000, 80 percent of it was paid for with Other People's Money— namely, the mortgage they got from the bank.) The Martins then took $20,000 in cash out of the equity they had accumulated in that little house and used it as a down payment on a second house that they eventually sold for $650,000. And so on. Even adding in all the mortgage payments they made along the way, the amount of money they put in was only a small fraction of the wealth they came to own—especially when you count all the rent their tenants paid them over the years. That's the power of leverage. A small amount of cash at the beginning can put you in a position to reap huge asset values down the road.

> ### STRATEGY NO. 2:
> ### DOWNSIZE TO THE RIGHT SIZE

I covered this approach in Chapter Two, when I shared the story of my friends in Las Vegas, Rick and Molly. You'll find it on pages 64 to 65. Reread it right now. Let it sink in. What this couple did is incredibly simple—yet most people don't do it. You could.

As I said earlier, what most people do when the value of their home goes up is to sell it and buy a bigger house with a bigger mortgage. The problem with this approach is that it doesn't make your life simpler. Rather, it usually makes it more expensive— more rooms to furnish, higher taxes to pay, richer neighbors to keep up with.

If you recall, the value of Rick and Molly's house jumped from $200,000 to $600,000 in just a few years. Now I know this is a best-case example, but how they decided to handle it demonstrates something important. Rather than simply sell their suddenly pricey home and use the windfall to buy a bigger house on a golf course with a bigger mortgage, they decided to use their equity to leverage their wealth and keep their life simple.

After they sold their house for $600,000, they took the $400,000 profit they made and used it to buy three new houses. First, they made a $75,000 down payment on what would be their new home—a $350,000 house in a community that was slightly less fancy than the one in which they had been living. They "downsized." This left them with a $275,000 mortgage, which at $1,650 a month was only a little bit more than what they had been paying on their old place. Then they took the remaining $325,000 profit and used it to make down payments on two other $300,000 houses that they planned to use as rental properties. Because they were able to make such large down payments on these houses (around $150,000 each), the mortgage payments were relatively low (just $900 a month each), and they were easily able to rent them out for enough to generate positive cash flow from Day One. In fact, the extra cash the two rental properties threw off paid for the higher cost of the mortgage on their new home. So there they were, spending less than the $1,300 a month it had cost them to live in their original $200,000 house— but now owning three homes worth nearly $1 million!

Again, we see the power of leverage— making the same amount of money go five times as far.

> ### STRATEGY NO. 3:
> ## CASH OUT AND INVEST ELSEWHERE

This is probably the most straightforward approach to building wealth through home-ownership. When your house goes up in value, you sell it and use part of the tax-free profits to put a down payment on a new house (with a new mortgage), and you put the rest of your profits in the bank. Then you wait until your new house appreciates and you do it again, and watch your bank balance grow.

Why is this such a phenomenally good deal? As I noted earlier, the government allows you to sell your home **without having to pay any taxes on the profits,** up to certain limits. If you are single, you can pocket up to $250,000 tax-free; if you are married, the ceiling is $500,000. And you can do this as often as once every two years. The rule says that to qualify for the exemption, you simply have to have lived in the house you're selling for two of the previous five years.

To see how this works, let's use Rick and Molly as an example. Had they not wanted to be landlords, they could have taken their $400,000 in tax-free profits and used $120,000 of it for a 20 percent down payment on another $600,000 house. The remaining $280,000 would have been gravy— free money to be used as they wished (though I would hope they would invest it for their future).

If property values continued to rise (which they've been doing in Las Vegas at an astonishing clip) and their new house eventually came to be worth $1 million, they could then sell it and take another $400,000 in tax-free profits.

In the kind of bull market we saw in real estate during the first five years of the twenty-first century, countless homeowners used this approach to build wealth tax-free. It requires you to stay on top of the real estate market in your area and move more frequently, but it can and does work. Of course, if and when real estate markets cool down, this strategy will take much longer to achieve results. But given the long-term upward trend in real estate values, its ultimate success is usually a matter of when, not if.

> ### STRATEGY NO. 4:
> ### BUY UP TO THE
> ### NEXT NEIGHBORHOOD

This is probably the most common approach to real estate investing. You buy a home, live in it for a while, grow your family—and your income—and then eventually move to a bigger home in a better neighborhood.

This ultimately creates leverage for you because you are now living in a more expensive home, and as it appreciates in value, your equity grows faster. (After all, while a 6 percent increase in the value of a $100,000 home will add $6,000 to its owner's equity, the same rise in the value of a $1 million home will make its owner $60,000 richer.)

I'm a classic example of this. Even though I procrastinated in the beginning, I eventually went from my first house—a $220,000 fixer-upper in the suburbs—to a $640,000 condo in San Francisco to a $2 million loft in New York that, as of this writing, is easily worth $3 million. The market could drop, of course, but at this point chances are that the loft is always going to be worth more than we paid for it.

The point is that at each step, the profits I made from the appreciation of my old home allowed me to buy a much more expensive new home. In this way, even without getting into the rental game, I've been able to buy three homes over the last 15 years—and in the process, increase my net worth by well over $1 million.

At this point, we could sell our loft and leverage up yet again. We just looked at a penthouse in a new development that would cost us $3.5 million. It's slightly smaller than our current place, but the building is new and "hot." My guess is that this new property has more upside than our current home. Probably a lot more upside.

So should we take another ride on the leverage express? It's what a lot of people do.

In the end, it's a personal decision. What you need to consider with this approach is that as you leverage up, your life becomes more expensive and often more complicated. Your apartment is more expensive, your neighborhood is more expensive, and your overhead just keeps getting bigger.

THINK ABOUT WHAT THE MARTINS DID

I'm not sharing any of this to brag. I'm sharing it to show you how simple homeownership simply builds tremendous wealth. It took me a decade of hard work to save $1 million. It took me 36 months to increase my net worth by another $1 million by simply being a homeowner in a hot market. We could have been renting a loft in New York this whole time and not made a cent. I'd say half of my friends in New York are doing just that. They thought we were crazy to buy in 2002—because the real estate market in New York supposedly couldn't get any hotter than it was then.

If you go back to the Martins for a second, remember that they also traded up three times. They went from a $30,000 home to a $100,000 home to a $750,000 home. When they sold that last house, it was worth $2 million. Then they stopped—and downsized to the right size. They bought a new, smaller home in a less-expensive area in Arizona. And they used some of their profits to buy a four-plex rental from which they now earn $90,000 a year in positive cash flow.

IT MAY SOUND TOO EASY TO BE TRUE, BUT IT REALLY DOES WORK

As you read this, the strategies I'm discussing and the stories I'm telling may seem too simple. If it's that easy, why isn't everyone rich? But keep one thing in mind. **None of this stuff just happens. You have to take action.**

The Martins didn't just happen to acquire their multimillion-dollar net worth. They didn't just accidentally become Automatic Millionaire Homeowners. They made a series of decisions at various points in their life that at times were scary. Their first home purchase, for only $30,000, was scary. They really didn't think they could afford it. Their rent was low, the neighborhood where they could afford to buy was not ideal, and they could have easily just kept renting. But they went for it.

When they decided to rent out their first home, they were scared. They didn't know if they would like being landlords. It wasn't all easy. Not all their tenants were perfect. They toughed it out, however, and never got rid of that first property.

They also were scared when they bought bigger and more expensive homes. Buying that $750,000 dream home of theirs was a huge decision. They never thought that it would go up in value the way it did. And there were plenty of times they thought they had over-extended themselves.

I can relate. When we bought our Tribeca loft I was plenty nervous. Ask my wife, Michelle. We were the first people to buy in our building—on the first day. Half the condos sold in a week. Then the New York real estate market started to slow. For six months, it literally just froze. Every week, the developer of my building would reduce his prices. The last condos to sell went for as much as $250,000 below their original price. By the end of those six months, the loft we had bought for $2,000,000 was probably worth $500,000 less than what we'd paid for it. If we had to sell it then, we could have lost a lot of our equity.

But we stayed put. The Martins stayed put. Things worked out. They often do.

As the Martins' dream home soared in value from $750,000 to $2 million, they decided to continue their journey. They looked at retirement communities where living costs were cheaper. They investigated Arizona. Many of their California friends thought they were crazy. "Move to the desert?" they said. "What are you thinking?"

What they were thinking was that they wanted to retire, and to do that they needed to reduce their overhead. "Let's use our real estate profits," they said to each other, "and retire early."

Which is what they did. But they were

scared when they did it. They didn't know they would like Arizona (which is why they rented there for a year before buying).

And they were scared to buy a four-plex as an investment property.

But it all worked out.

NOTHING GREAT IS EVER EASY—AND IT'S ALMOST ALWAYS SCARY

My point is this: Nothing I've shared with you in this book is risk-free. The same can be said of my experience. It may be simple, but it's not easy.

Let me say that again. **Getting rich through homeownership may be simple, but it's not always easy.** You can take this chapter and read it ten times. Not one of these ideas will ever be a "no brainer" for you. You will have to stretch your comfort level if you're going to do anything more than simply buy a house and live it in for the rest of your life.

Of course, if that's all you do—just buy

a house, pay it down early, and live in it for the rest of your life while its value appreciates—**that's still a lot better than renting for the rest of your life and making someone else rich!**

AUTOMATIC MILLIONAIRE HOMEOWNER ACTION STEPS

Reviewing the actions we laid out in this chapter, here's what you should be doing right now to go from being an ordinary homeowner to an Automatic Millionaire Homeowner.

❑ Re-read the story of John and Lucy Martin in Chapter One and start thinking of your home not simply as a place to live in but as a vehicle for building wealth.

❑ Check to see if rents in your area for a house like yours are high enough for you to consider becoming a landlord.

❑ Calculate how much equity you have in your house and consider a cash-out refinancing, a series of sales with tax-free profits, or "leveraging up."

❑ Above all, commit to taking action.

❑ Go to **www.finishrich.com/ homeowner/chapterten** to listen to the free audio supplement to this chapter.

CHAPTER ELEVEN

HOW TO "BUBBLE-PROOF" YOUR REAL ESTATE PLAN— AND SURVIVE A DOWNTURN

For the previous ten chapters, I've been encouraging you to go out and buy a home because it will ultimately be the best investment you ever make. So why switch the focus now to the downside of real estate? Well, the fact is that real estate has cycles. Just like the stock market, real estate prices don't always go up. The fact is, they can go down.

I've been around the business long

enough to remember the real estate boom of the early 1980s, and I remember the California real estate crash that followed it in the late 1980s. My first job after I graduated from the University of Southern California in 1990 was as a commercial real estate agent in Pleasanton, California, where I had the privilege of working on some of the largest corporate accounts in northern California (including companies like Pacific Bell, AT&T, and Prudential). From 1990 to 1993, I worked on tens of millions of dollars' worth of leases and commercial sales. I remember doing a search for 500,000 square feet of office space for one of our clients. We wound up touring more than 15 buildings in the Bay Area—all of them empty!

"What happened here?" I asked my boss. "How can there be so many buildings of this size sitting around empty?"

"It's called a down cycle," he replied. "It happens every 20 years. Developers overbuild, banks overloan, people get overexcited and overextend. They all think the good times will go on forever, but they don't."

He was right. Inevitably, any boom will bust. It happens over and over again, but no one ever seems to learn.

THE RESIDENTIAL MARKET WASN'T ANY BETTER

If you had bought a home at the peak of the California real estate market in the late 1980s, it would be nearly a decade before your house would once again be worth what you probably paid for it. As a result, many, many people who for one reason or another had to sell their houses during this period were forced into bankruptcy because they couldn't get the price they had paid. They ended up owing more than their properties were worth—and often had no choice but simply to give their houses back to the bank.

As I write this in July 2005, after 13 straight years of steady—and, in some cases, startling—increases in home prices, cracks are beginning to show in the real estate market. There are signs—at least in certain parts of the country—that things may be cooling off.

It's getting scary. With some experts predicting what could be a brutal real estate meltdown, you need to protect yourself.

Here's how you can do that.

FIVE SIMPLE WAYS TO PROTECT YOURSELF FROM A REAL ESTATE MELTDOWN

1. MAKE SURE YOU CAN AFFORD YOUR MORTGAGE

This book is primarily about building wealth through homeownership. That means owning the house you live in or rent out. Not the house you buy just to flip. The buy-and-flip book is someone else's. What we're talking about here is the commonsense approach to building your wealth through homeownership.

What does that mean? Well, to begin

with, it means not buying a house you can't really afford.

You may not be able to afford your home if . . .

- You put nothing down.
- You took out an interest-only mortgage.
- You took an option mortgage, and you are paying the minimum allowed (resulting in negative amortization).
- You don't have a savings "cushion" big enough to cover several months' worth of mortgage payments.

I'm not saying you shouldn't buy a home if any of these things apply to you. As we saw in John and Lucy Martin's story, there's nothing wrong with stretching a little in order to become a homeowner. It certainly beats continuing to rent. BUT you should still be sensible, which means regarding those signs I just listed as "red flags." If any of them apply to you, it means you are taking a risk when you buy a home in a booming real estate market.

According to SMR Research, one out of three homebuyers in 2004 took out adjustable rate or interest-only mortgages, and more than 70 percent of them borrowed more than 80 percent of the purchase price. According to the National Association of Realtors, 40 percent put down no money at all.

This sort of thing works fine when real estate values are going up and interest rates stay low. But when interest rates skyrocket and home prices drop—both of which are very real possibilities—you end up with a "double whammy." People who bought homes they couldn't really afford are suddenly in trouble because their mortgage payments are jumping by 50 percent to 75 percent. But they can't sell because, with prices dropping, their homes are now worth less than they owe on them.

This stuff happens. In fact, it happens almost predictably—coming around just like a comet about every twenty years.

So what should you do?

BUBBLE-PROOF YOUR PROPERTY

Here are six ways you can protect yourself.

- Lock in your mortgage interest rate—ideally, by getting a 30-year or 15-year fixed-rate mortgage.
- If you have an adjustable mortgage, refinance while rates are still low and lock in the rate for at least five years—the longer the better. Even if you're planning to sell in fewer than five years, lock in your rate for a longer period to protect yourself in case you run into a down cycle during which selling may not make sense.
- Pay a little extra on your mortgage every month so that your principal balance shrinks as quickly as possible.
- If you have an interest-only mortgage, start paying off some of the principal.
- Use your equity in your home wisely. My recommendation is that you use equity to build your assets, not "bor-

row them." Specifically, borrow your equity out of your house to buy more real estate, improve your current home—or buy more assets. Be careful about using your equity to pay off credit cards, take a vacation, buy a car, or for day-to-day expenses.

• Start building an emergency savings account; aim to have six months' worth of housing costs in the bank—and Make It Automatic!

2. THINK LOCAL

At the end of the day, the only real estate market that should matter to you is the one you are in! Real estate is talked about a lot nationally—as in "the national average home price went up over 50 percent in five years." **What the market does nationally is irrelevant to you.** What you care about is the value of your house or condo, which literally can depend on which street you live on or which building you live in. If your home is in Columbus, Ohio, what's happening in the Miami condo market is pretty much meaningless, unless you happen also to own a condo in Miami.

Here's how to keep on top of **your** real estate market:

READ ABOUT AND DRIVE THE MARKET

Open the local newspaper and look at the real estate section. Are there homes like yours for sale? Are there a lot of them? Check out the paper every week. Does it look like the same homes are for sale week after week, month after month? Are they moving or not?

Next, drive around your neighborhood looking for "For Sale" signs. Are they everywhere—or are there only a few? Again, does it look like homes are selling?

VISIT OPEN HOUSES

The best way to get a quick feel for the pulse of your market is to visit open houses on the weekend. Are they packed with people looking to buy? Ask the real estate agents hosting the open houses, "How's the market?" After you've spoken to a half dozen of them over the course of a single Saturday afternoon, you should have a pretty good sense of what's going on in your area.

If the market is tight and houses are selling, you can relax. If not, you should prepare for a down cycle—meaning you should take care not to overextend yourself, watch your expenses carefully, and try your best to avoid a situation where you may be forced to sell.

3. GET THE FACTS

When you own (or are thinking of buying) an investment property, there are a handful of really important things you should know about your market: what the housing inventory is like, where prices are going, and how long homes are sitting on the market. The fastest way to get this information is to meet with a great real estate agent who specializes in your neighborhood. You learned how to do that in Chapter Eight. Here are some key questions to ask that agent to find out what's happening in your local marketplace:

Inventory: How many homes like yours are for sale in the area? The key phrase here is "homes like yours." It doesn't matter if there are fifty homes for sale in your neighborhood if only five are like yours. You need to compare what's in the market that's the same size, age, quality, and style as your home with the total number of homes for sale. If an appreciable fraction (say, more than 15 percent or 20 percent) is very similar to your home, you may face a challenge getting top dollar.

Prices: What are homes like yours selling for? Earlier, we discussed the importance of getting the "comps." If you're thinking about selling in the near future, ask your real estate agent to give you monthly updates on sale prices of comparable homes.

Time on the market: When a home goes on the market, the selling agent tracks how many days it takes to find a buyer. These numbers are looked at both nationally and locally as a key indicator of whether a market is heating up or cooling down. Obviously, the longer it takes to sell a home, the cooler the market is. Of course, this is just one indicator, and it often gets skewed by anomalies— a home that sells in a day or one that sits unsold for a year. Still, you want to know what's happening in your area. Are homes moving fast or moving slower?

4. DON'T BUY A HOUSE OR CONDO JUST TO "FLIP" IT

This book is about investing—about buying a home and using it as the foundation of your financial security. If you buy a rental property, it has to be capable of generating positive cash flow. If that's not a reasonable expectation, then you shouldn't buy it. And even if you're confident a property will fetch a high enough rent to cover the costs, you still shouldn't buy it if you don't have at least three months' worth of mortgage payments in the bank— just in case it takes you a while to find a tenant.

Most important of all, don't go out in a hot market and buy a new condo in a new building that's not yet built in the hope that you will be able to "flip" it for a quick and easy profit. You may buy a flip and end up flopping—particularly if you buy in a booming market with new condo towers going up on every block. A few months or years down the road, when the market is flooded with these new condos, and everyone else is hoping to flip theirs, you could easily find yourself with a real challenge. And don't assume that if you can't sell, you'll be able to "just rent it out." The rental market falls, too. When there are more condos going up than there are people buying, rents will decline. More likely, you'll find yourself stuck with mortgage payments you can't afford. So think seriously about this before you just leap in.

With any investment, the best time to leap into a hot market may be after it's cooled and others are scrambling to sell.

5. KNOW THAT, IN MOST CASES, TIME CURES ALL

The one great certainty with real estate is that, over the long term, "time cures all"—at least in most cases. What this means is that areas that go bust eventually come back. Every great city has had its bleak periods, but invariably they recover from them.

New York City in the 1970s was brutal. Then it boomed in the early 1980s. And then it went bust again. By the early 1990s, you couldn't give away a condo there. I remember a friend of mine who bought a brand new, three-bedroom condo on the upper East Side back then for $180,000. Her dad loaned her the down payment and said, "Get some friends to rent the other two bedrooms. In a decade, you'll be rich."

We all thought he was crazy. Well, today that condo is worth well over $2 million. New York City real estate came back with a vengeance. The same is true of markets all over the country, from Miami to Houston to San Diego. Markets boom, then go bust, then boom again.

In the end, what matters is whether you have the resources to ride out the cycle. If your time frame is short and you buy near the end of an up cycle, there's a good chance you're going to get hurt. But if you can hang on for the long haul—say, at least seven years, which is the average length of time Americans own their homes—you shouldn't have anything to worry about, even if the bubble in your area pops.

Remember—being an Automatic Millionaire Homeowner isn't about timing the market. **It's about time in the market. It's when you're NOT trying to get rich quick that you get rich slowly.**

AUTOMATIC MILLIONAIRE HOMEOWNER ACTION STEPS

Reviewing the actions we laid out in this chapter, here's what you should be doing right now to "bubble-proof" your real estate plan.

❑ Make sure you can afford your mortgage.

❑ Find out what's selling and for how much in your neighborhood.

❑ Don't try to make a "quick killing." Think long-term.

❑ Make sure you have the resources to ride out the real estate cycle.

❑ Go to **www.finishrich.com/ homeowner/chaptereleven** to listen to the free audio supplement to this chapter.

CHAPTER TWELVE

MAKE A DIFFERENCE— HELP SOMEONE ELSE BECOME A HOMEOWNER

We've spent the last few hours looking at how you can build a foundation for real wealth through homeownership. Becoming an **Automatic Millionaire Homeowner** is now truly within your reach. Indeed, I hope you've already begun your journey. If not, I hope that when you put this book down, you'll be inspired to start making it happen. But before we end our time together, I want to share one more idea—one additional thing you can do to change your life for the better.

HAPPINESS BEGINS WITH GIVING

Many people read my books and become inspired to make their lives richer and more secure. That's certainly my goal, but I also want to inspire my readers to help others. When I wrote **The Automatic Millionaire** (the book that led to this one), I ended it with a chapter called "Give Back Automatically." This chapter was about the importance of helping others and the power of making that kind of giving automatic. It shared the message of how giving back to others a piece of what we bring in for ourselves can make the world a better place.

This is something I believe with all my heart. The fact is, there is more to life than money. Now this may strike you as a strange thing to read in a book about how to be-

come a millionaire through homeownership. But it's true. In fact, not only is it true,
it is also important.

Now don't get me wrong. Money is good,
and I sincerely hope you get the riches you
want. But money will not give your life
meaning.

What will is giving something back. As I
see it, the only reason to learn how to make
more money and build wealth is ultimately
to be able to help others. We are put here to
make the world a better place. And here's
something amazing. Although you should
give simply for the sake of giving, the reality
is that abundance tends to flow back to
those who give. **The more you give, the
more comes back to you. It is the flow of
abundance that brings us more joy, more
love, more wealth, and more meaning in
our lives.**

After **The Automatic Millionaire** was
published, countless readers wrote to tell
me that this final chapter was what ultimately inspired them to become Automatic
Millionaires—that what got them moti-

vated was not simply the idea of having more but the idea of being able to give more.

I share this story because I want to end this book in a similar way—by teaching you how you can give something back as an Automatic Millionaire Homeowner. After you've become a homeowner (or, indeed, while you're in the process of doing it), there is an extremely practical and effective way you can help others do the same—and I'd like to make sure you know about it.

A GREAT WAY TO HELP OTHERS GET A HOME AND BUILD A FUTURE

If, after having read this book, you believe as I do that the best route to personal financial security is through homeownership, then you should also believe that one of the best ways to end poverty would be to find a way to put even those who can't afford it into their own homes. Estimates put the number of American families unable to find decent housing they can afford at more than 5 million—and that's not counting the impact of Hurricanes Katrina and Rita, which displaced more than a million Gulf Coast residents and damaged or destroyed hundreds of thousands of homes throughout Louisiana, Mississippi, and Alabama in 2005. Helping all these people find homes may seem like an impossible goal, but it's not. In fact, there are numerous charitable organizations doing just this every day.

HOW YOU CAN HELP

If the idea of helping someone else get into a home appeals to you, there are literally hundreds of organizations to which you can contribute both time and money. I've listed six really worthy ones below, but they are just the tip of the iceberg. Do some research of your own through web sites like Charity Navigator (**www.charitynavigator.org**) or Guidestar (**www.guidestar.org**), and find a group in your own community that could use your help.

Corporation for Supportive Housing
50 Broadway
17th Floor
New York, NY 10004
www.csh.org
1-212-986-2966

The Corporation for Supportive Housing (CSH) provides professional advice and development expertise as well as loans and grants to local communities, with the aim of ending homelessness by creating permanent housing that includes the kind of support systems many homeless people need to deal with their underlying problems (such as disabilities, substance abuse, and mental illness). Since its founding in 1991, CSH has helped create some 14,437 units of supportive housing—and aims to create another 150,000 units over the next ten years.

Habitat for Humanity International
121 Habitat
St. Americus, GA 31709-3498
www.habitat.org
1-229-924-6935, ext. 2551 or 2552

Since 1976, Habitat for Humanity has helped build more than 200,000 homes in upward of 100 countries around the world—sheltering more than 1 million people in some 3,000 communities worldwide. The basic philosophy isn't to give homes away to anyone, but to give poor people who are willing to work hard a chance to earn the homes they need and deserve. In the United States, Habitat for Humanity builds or renovates homes, then helps low-income families (generally those with incomes 30 percent to 50 percent below the median for their area) buy them with no-interest loans and down payments as modest as $500. But need alone is not enough to qualify for a Habitat house. The family must also contribute substantial "sweat equity," typically putting in 300 to 500 hours helping to build or renovate their home or someone else's. As a volunteer, you literally raise the frames and pound the nails to help make it possible for a family to one day sleep under their own roof.

Local Initiatives Support Corporation

501 Seventh Avenue
7th Floor
New York, NY 10018
www.lisc.org
1-212-455-9800

The Local Initiatives Support Corporation helps local groups improve distressed neighborhoods throughout the country by providing Community Development Corporations with capital, technical expertise, and training. A key part of LISC's mission is developing affordable housing through its Center for Home-Ownership, Housing Authority Resource Center, and Affordable Housing Preservation Initiative.

The Housing Assistance Council
1025 Vermont Ave., NW
Suite 606
Washington, DC 20005
www.ruralhome.org
1-202-842-8600

Emphasizing local solutions, reduced dependence, and self-help, the Housing Assistance Council (HAC) has been helping local organizations build affordable homes in rural America since 1971. It promotes homeownership for working low-income rural families through a "sweat equity" approach similar to Habitat for Humanity's, with a special focus on high-need groups in Native American communities, the Mississippi Delta, the Southwest border **colonias**, and Appalachia.

National Alliance to End Homelessness
1518 K Street NW, Suite 410
Washington, DC 20005
www.endhomelessness.org
1-202-638-1526

The National Alliance to End Homelessness is a nonprofit organization whose mission is to mobilize the nonprofit, public, and private sectors of society in an alliance to end homelessness. Its "Ten Year Plan to End Homelessness" aims to identify the root causes of the problem and lays out practical steps to solve it over the next decade.

Rebuilding Together
1536 Sixteenth Street NW
Washington, DC 20036
www.rebuildingtogether.org
1-800-473-4229

Founded in 1988, Rebuilding Together works to preserve and revitalize houses for low-income homeowners. Over the last 16 years, some 2.3 million Rebuilding Together volunteers have helped to rehabilitate 87,450 homes and nonprofit facilities.

NOW MAKE IT AUTOMATIC

If you decide to contribute your sweat equity by volunteering for an organization like Habitat for Humanity or Rebuilding Together, more power to you. But if you decide to make a financial contribution to one of the charities listed here, make up your mind to Make It Automatic. Many charities encourage people to become regular supporters by contributing a small amount monthly, using an automatic funds transfer.

Homeownership lets you get rich where you sleep. Automatic giving lets you help others while you sleep.

WHAT I'M DOING TO HELP OTHERS

Because I think it is so important that we help others become financially secure through homeownership, I'm marking the publication of this book with a $50,000 donation from my FinishRich Foundation to Habitat for Humanity. Habitat will also be getting a portion of the royalties from every copy of this book sold in the United States in 2006. So if you're thinking about buying a copy of this book for a friend, keep in mind that a portion of the sales price will be going to help a needy family get a home of their own.

JOIN THE GREAT AMERICAN HOMEOWNER CHALLENGE™

The publication of this book is really just the beginning of my mission to help renters become homeowners. I believe so strongly that the secret to financial independence and security is homeownership that I will be touring America after the publication of this book, hosting FREE educational events as part of what we're calling **The Great American Homeowner Challenge.** This initiative will be focused on helping anyone who wants to buy a home get into a home. Specifically, we are working to inspire 10 million people to buy homes over the next ten years.

I hope this book has inspired you—and that you will join us at an event. Visit our web site (**www.finishrich.com**) for details on when I'll be in your area.

TELL A FRIEND— SHARE THE DREAM!

I hope you close this book inspired to make homeowner-ship your path to financial freedom. Nothing helps you achieve success faster than helping others. So please consider sharing what you've learned in this book with someone you love—particularly if they are still a renter. Lend this book to them. Suggest they take it out from the library. Pass along some of the e-mail links to my free audios on homeownership.

If you want to buy a copy of this book for friend, that's great—but please know that my goal isn't simply to sell more books. It's to share the message. And the best way I know to do that is for you to live what you learn and prove it works.

Together, we can really make a difference.

YOUR JOURNEY HOME BEGINS TODAY!

I want you to know that I am proud of you for coming so far in this journey. You bought this book—and you read it! Well done. Now go use what you've learned to make your life the way you want and the world the way it can be.

This book was written to be a simple guide filled with simple ideas about how you can become an Automatic Millionaire Homeowner. I've tried to make it as power-

ful and action-oriented as possible, to arm
you with ideas, strategies, and action steps
designed to get you going on the road to
wealth and financial security through homeownership.

But you must "get going." And you
should do it today.

The one thing I know for sure is that, over
the long term, real estate prices are going
up. Maybe not tomorrow or next year—
but long-term, they are going up. They
always have.

Even if the real estate markets cool, I
promise that twenty years from now you'll
look back and think, "Wow, I can't believe
how cheap that property was twenty years
ago!"

Remember—**as long as you're alive,
you have to live somewhere.** So does everyone else you know. And because of that,
homeownership will continue to be a great
investment.

SO NOW IT'S UP TO YOU

You are an amazing person. Deep down inside, you know you can do this. So go do it.

Don't let the markets, the difficulties, or the skeptics keep you from going for your dreams.

If you are renting and want to own a home—go make it happen.

If you own a home and want to own a bigger home—go make it happen.

If you want to own rental properties—go make it happen.

And if you want to give back—**GO MAKE IT HAPPEN!**

Your life is short. Live it to its fullest. **Live it rich.**

ACKNOWLEDGMENTS

To everyone who has helped FinishRich Media and me help others live and finish rich, I say a heartfelt and humble THANK YOU!

The Automatic Millionaire Homeowner is the eighth book I've written in the FinishRich Series® in the last eight years. There are currently more than 4 million FinishRich books in print, translated into fifteen languages in more than forty countries. As our message spreads around the world, it is important to point out that I couldn't possibly have done this by myself. It takes a great team of great people to make a difference—and what follows is only a partial list of the many people who have helped us help others.

First, to my loyal readers—you really are why I do what I do. Your success energizes me and our team at FinishRich Media to wake up every day and help you to live a great life. To those of you who have sent us letters, e-mails, and notes, come to our seminars or attended our coaching programs, and helped share the message, "Thank you, thank you, thank you." We will keep working hard to answer your questions and give you what you need to live and finish rich.

To my team at FinishRich Media, which is growing every day, thank you for working so hard to spread our mission. To Nicola Zahn, Unity Stoakes, Stephanie Oakes, Liz Dougherty, Susan Zimmerman, Andy DiSimone, Gabriella Weiser—you make coming to work fun. To Nicola Zahn—what can I say? You've traveled to more than sixty cities with me in less than a year, and you still smile at me! Thank you for keeping my life sane, my projects organized, and my spirits high. You are as wonderful to work with as anyone I have ever met, and I feel blessed on a daily basis that you came into my life.

To my team outside FinishRich Media, thank you!

To Allan Mayer—we've now done six books together. This one was harder than most, yet you made it all seem easy. You are as good as they come and a total joy to work with. Your suggestions and edits and overall guidance in shaping this book (especially the 10,000 words you cut) made it what it is. Thank you—I really consider ours a world-class partnership.

To Jan Miller and Shannon Miser Marvin—thank you for what is now nearly a decade of representing me through the thick and thin of the publishing world. Your guidance has been immeasurable. Your promises have all come true. I both admire and love you ladies.

To Stephen Breimer—what a year we've had. Thank you for saying "no" when I wanted to say "yes"—and for protecting me on deal after deal. You are as good as they come in the legal profession, and as good as they come as a person. Thank you!

To my team at Doubleday Broadway Group—I love you guys. Most authors go from publisher to publisher. I've stayed with you since 1997, and I'm grateful that I have. You've worked diligently to grow my brand and protect its quality and integrity. To Kris

Puopolo—you are a dream editor, and I know it! I sing your praises every day because I know your feedback is invaluable, brilliant—and right. Thank you for truly being both dedicated and interested in my books, their mission, and their message. You are my best reader—and because of that our readers are blessed. To my publisher, Stephen Rubin—I feel lucky to have the direct honest relationship we have. You make publishing enjoyable. To David Drake—gosh, eight books and counting. Who would have believed one could have a publicist for nearly a decade! You are just incredible. This will be our biggest book yet. To the sales and publishing team at Doubleday Broadway Group—Michael Palgon, Janelle Moburg, Janet Cooke, and so many more—you do the work that makes it all happen. To Catherine Pollack and Judy Jacoby, thank you for your brilliant guidance on marketing and advertising. To Jean Traina, thanks for making this cover fantastic and for listening patiently to all my suggestions and changes. I love the results!

To my family and friends—I'm officially

apologizing. I'm sorry that my life has become so busy that I rarely see you, but I hope you know I love you! Thank you for continuing to call me, e-mail me, join me on the road—and visit me in New York. I miss you more than you know. To Mom and Dad (Bobbi and Marty Bach), the parents of all parents—you are just the best! No kid could be luckier. To my little sis, Emily—I love you!

To our sponsors of **The Great American Homeowner Challenge**™—in particular, Wells Fargo Home Mortgage, which came to the table first and said, "We want to help you reach 10 million people"—THANK YOU! A special "thank you" to Nancy Brennan, Cara Heiden, and Lisa Zakrajsek for carrying the torch to the "starting line." Our mission in 2006 is to empower those millions of people, and I'm so excited that we'll be working together.

To our team at Yahoo—thank you for our partnership on **The Automatic Millionaire** column. What a blast it is to share our message with the world every two weeks through your platform.

To my wife, Michelle, and my two-year-old son, Jack—I love you so much! Jack, I promise that your daddy will be hanging with you at the park this year. Michelle, I'm really sorry. I promised you that after a year on the road I would spend the summer with you at the beach and relax, and instead I spent much of it in the library writing this book. Thank you for understanding. I promise to spend **this** summer at the beach with you and not in the library on book number nine.

Finally, to YOU reading this book—while we have not yet met personally, I feel like I know you and I thank you for being interested in my message of hope and prosperity and my mission to make a difference. I'm so grateful that you gave me the chance to be your coach, and I hope that we do get to meet face to face someday along the journey.

Live Rich,
David Bach
New York
November 2005

ABOUT DAVID BACH

David Bach has helped millions of people around the world take action to live and finish rich. He is the author of six consecutive national bestsellers, including two consecutive #1 **New York Times** bestsellers, **Start Late, Finish Rich** and **The Automatic Millionaire,** as well as the national and international bestsellers **Smart Women Finish Rich, Smart Couples Finish Rich, The Finish Rich Workbook,** and **The Automatic Millionaire Workbook.** Bach carries the unique distinction of having had four of his books appear simultaneously on the

Wall Street Journal, Business Week, and **USA Today** bestseller lists. In addition, four of Bach's books were named to **USA Today's** Best Sellers of the Year list for 2004. In all, his FinishRich Books have been published in more than 15 languages, with more than three million copies in print worldwide.

Bach's breakout book **The Automatic Millionaire** was the #1 Business book of 2004, according to **Business Week**. It spent fourteen weeks on the **New York Times** bestseller list and was simultaneously number one on the bestseller lists of the **New York Times, Business Week, USA Today,** and the **Wall Street Journal.** With over a million copies in print, this simple powerful book has been translated into twelve languages and has inspired thousands around the world to save money automatically.

Bach is also the author of **1001 Financial Words You Need to Know: The Ultimate Guide to the Language of Business and Finance,** published by Oxford University Press.

Bach is regularly featured on television and radio as well as in newspapers and magazines. He has appeared twice on **The Oprah Winfrey Show** to share his strategies for living and finishing rich. He has been a regular contributor to CNN's **American Morning** and has appeared frequently on ABC's **The View,** NBC's **Today** and **Weekend Today** shows, CBS's **Early Show,** Fox News Channel's **The O'Reilly Factor,** CNBC's **Power Lunch,** CNNfn, and MSNBC and **The Big Idea with Donny Deutsch.** He has been profiled in numerous major publications, including **The New York Times, Business Week, USA Today, People, Reader's Digest, Time, Financial Times,** the **Washington Post,** the **Wall Street Journal, Los Angeles Times, San Francisco Chronicle, Working Woman, Glamour, Redbook,** and **Family Circle.** He is a featured contributor and columnist at Yahoo!, where his column **"The Automatic Millionaire with David Bach"** appears biweekly.

David Bach is the creator of the FinishRich® Seminar series, which highlights his quick and easy-to-follow financial strategies. In just the last few years, more than half a million people have learned how to take financial action to live a life in line with their values by attending his Smart Women Finish Rich®, Smart Couples Finish Rich®, and Find the Money Seminars, which have been taught in more than 2,000 cities throughout North America by thousands of financial advisors.

A renowned financial speaker, Bach regularly presents seminars for and delivers keynote addresses to the world's leading financial service firms, Fortune 500 companies, universities, and national conferences. He is the founder and Chairman of FinishRich Media, a company dedicated to revolutionizing the way people learn about money. Prior to founding FinishRich Media, he was a senior vice president of Morgan Stanley and a partner of The Bach Group, which during his tenure (1993 to 2001) managed more than half a billion dollars for individual investors.

David Bach lives with his wife, Michelle, and son, Jack, in New York, where he is currently working on his ninth book, **Start Young, Finish Rich.** Please visit his web site at **www.finishrich.com.**

LIKE WHAT YOU'VE SEEN?

If you enjoyed this large print edition of THE
AUTOMATIC MILLIONAIRE HOMEOWNER, look
for *START LATE, FINISH RICH* by David Bach,
available from Random House Large Print.

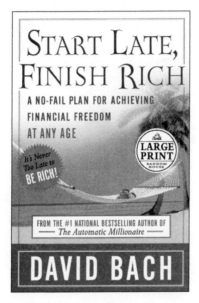

START LATE, FINISH RICH
(hardcover)
0-375-43464-X • $27.00/$38.00C

Large print books are available wherever books
are sold and at many local libraries.